This wisdom is to be shared with everyone!

It is time to learn how to protect the carnal spirit from itself: nothing missing or broke.

This may not be a best seller but it is a help to stop the killing. You may even find some bad grammar and misspelled words. Please overlook them.

Help to Stop Bullet Bullies

(Ending a part of Satan's Dieconomie)

#God said Enough Killing

Dedication

This book is dedicated to all who escape the dieconomie that Satan has set up for someone. I hope to help show as many people as I can that life is good and it is meant to be enjoyed.

This little book is a tip of the iceberg. To know more there is #Enough. This book is for all forms of ideology of people who may have an unnatural attraction to a weapon.

These books have different messages for many different age levels.

This book is one of the trinity of the books that are really showing people how the growth of beauty is inside of love.

Foreword

Hello and thank you for being in the present of this wisdom. Know that we are one of the countries that need to prevent death and this is one way!

To get things off on a sour note, this book may not be a book to like because it is not cutely written or edited. The subject matter is not very flattering but it is to be loved for the message it has a presence that lights a way out of darkness to be used by a multitude of people.

This is a way to help stop the child bully and adult bullet bully from becoming and remaining stuck in that way of life. This can be the help to not let the roots of Satan takes a hold of a child or it gives you the power to pull them out to keep people safe. This wisdom also stops the bullet bully sin-drome lifestyle.

What a blessing

Could this be the biggest uncollaring to take place in history to free mankind from Satan's dieconomie?

This is one of God's cease fire peace treaties to have with yourself regarding all others, no matter who or what it is about. The death angel or the grim reaper doesn't word when this treaty is called up   on in the heart of anyone with the loveoutame flower that creates a heavenly power that gives the control of one's self over to the angels in heaven to take charge of the life matters and stop the death matters concept of Satan.

The Lord is friending you. Are you willing to accept him? This is only another way he shows his love.

Let's agree that that Satan has bankrupted his account with us and this calls for a hallelujah.

To not become even more blinded in life, if you know someone who is making plastic guns tell an authority figure to help stop them from doing the wrong thing.

To make it known

Man put his conditions on other men and want them to follow them. God didn't say he put conditions on you after you accept him as savior in the ways mankind tries to. He only requires your obedience to his word.

I used to think it was an unfortunate thing for me to have the kind of responsibility I do on me but not anymore. It is a joy I find in my work for the Lord.

To understand to dig up to get out of something by passing the darkness and moving into the light is what the loveoutame does.

Ending the killing

If we start now we can be done with it by the time the Lord returns. If the Lord trusted you with something how would you do with the challenge?

M-N

The Lord wants us to know that this is a part of His glory that came down from Heaven that He wishes for us to use to bless each other.

To help stop the red blood shed mother earth is tired of feeling it, maybe that's why it's spilling out that volcano now in Hawaii, so much blood has ran down into the earth it is spitting it back up now in a different way.

If we understand how to stop the bloodshed maybe the volcano will stop, maybe this is a sign.

Information about what is in #Enough

One of the greatest things about becoming or attempting to becoming a hooded saint disciple is no matter how you're caught in one of Satan's zones or deep into the void-noid states, you can be whisk back into a solid state of being and put your feet on solid ground within a twinkling of an eye as quick as you may possibly think about getting out of the dangerous places that you are in. You can be out of them.

Every disciple should know

As things come down to the top side of this whole process, all clergy men and women are supposed to

4

have the presence of a un-hooded saint disciple in making sure that all mankind is aware of the dieconomie that Satan has been working with creating death in a multitude of ways. This is something that anyone who feels they are doing the will of God is supposed to be aware of. Now, also at the same time, it is a presence of you as a layman in the body of Christ can be awarded this state of growth too.

God is no respecter of persons when it comes down to presenting you with something of His when He has placed it in your heart to be a part of, so think not about moving forward on this pathway in any selfish way, but move forward in this pathway to show even greater love and growth towards your fellow man. Amen and Hallelujah.

Do you know there are some people who kill and really didn't want to? What happen is they fell under Satan's rule and got caught without the wisdom they need to stop themselves.

No one else has to get caught with their pants down to have to take an ass kicking like this again once they get this protection.

The main goal is getting as many people as possible in a better position of staying alive and if you are one thank the Lord.

To help make people aware of Satan who tries to trap people into all levels of addition to convince them to gamble with their lives in a dishonest state of drugs to cause them to overdose to add to Satan's dieconomie.

This is why we are renewed by this wake up call to get out of the system that wants to bury you so you can't share the love that you were born with inside to stop it from coming out all of the way. The more this is known or gets around the more it gets in Satan's way to stop him from doing duty crap.

Time to Know

To know the odyssey of the youth and the fact that bullies in school may seldom grow up to be bullet bullies they may be the ones who get or got bullied. It is my perception that the bullet bullies are the ones who have the conception of a towerist level of thinking even if it is on a gang of gangster principles of interest that intensified someone. The immaturity of the thought process has no grasp of this being a part of their existence.

That is why we look to explain and teach the newly developing thinkers as if we too are scientists who find new things in the universe, even if it is in the inner or invisible one some people don't believe in.

The way to not go

Even after all I said the part I want to forget about the most was when I was tempted to harm someone as was when I was going in and out of the bullet bully state of mind that I thank God it never took complete control of me. It was like a dark shadow came over me that took all of my feelings away of love and caring and concern for anyone. It is a feeling of emptiness and blindness as if the world left me behind. I couldn't stand being there or didn't want anyone else to be there it was like a kind of portal open up and the spirit wanted someone to go through it at a dark time.

The dislike for someone wasn't all it was about. It was the fact of feeling someone going through that exit. The negative energy that pulls on someone can become overwhelming. It is like a trick to a state of freedom that doesn't really need to be gone to but the unwise go there with actions because of pain others may cause or want to cause them, or they have it for themselves. The pain that hurts you comes from wanting to hurt someone and having pain I felt before on both levels. It is somewhat the same that wanted to cause me to open up a portal into death per-say for the hell of it. I am so thankful I didn't go there and I hope you never go there until it is your time or send someone else there before their time, thanks to the power of the loveoutame flower.

What is one of the greatest facts about life that can help people grow up more daily? It is to come to an understanding that you don't own anything in this world but your inner well-being. Furthermore, the best investment maybe to get the way of travel through life to help others understand this also regardless of the steps it takes to survive and make a living.

This can be a certificate to let all who have read and understood this guide a way to freedom. You have gone through the right of passage to not kill self or others. Furthermore, you have earned the wisdom to know as someone who can become a kind of lifeguard or a watchman for Christ at the least.

There is a book I would like you to I wrote titled: _A Calling to Become Watchman_. It is something that I came to understand the people who the demons of darkness want the most may be the ones that have the most to help others.

The people who Satan want to destroy most can be the ones who God chooses to lead others to the Promised Land that is found in the hearts of mankind at this time in history.

In real time value

This truth may be worth more than all the artwork at the Vatican in Rome. This is priceless also some of it can be taken with you after you leave this world. It is like a cake that has been baked in heaven and brought down to earth by an angel then given to mankind.

M-N

If I only get one book right for the readers it will be enough for me to be content with my work I have done for the Lord. Which one will be chosen by the people? I will take my time. One can be a life saver. One can be a life changer. One can be the one that helps someone make their life better. Therefore, how many ones do I need I say it again just one.

To not see darkness

When you think you have lost control and by doing something wrong it makes some people feel like they gain control. It is not true because to lose control and know your limit is okay. We are human and meant to be somewhat broken. It gets fixed from being in a troubled state of life. We can weather storms.

If you have taken notes you can keep this common sense reminder. There are people and places that may push your buttons and make you feel uncomfortable. I will say it only once in this book, even if you are licensed to carry you may feel the finger itch factor.

Stay away from those who may be haters that don't know they are. Everyone you may come across in life may not know the things you know. So don't brag on what you know. Show what you know with love.

That is why you have to be the adult and not the kid in ways that some people haven't grown up out of yet, unfortunately.

M-N

The intervention of this process is to set up a new kind of growth mindset to go to every time it is needed. It is always nice to have a place to succumb to.

M-N

This is an anti-weaponizing franchise

of positive energy in love that is priceless.

Foresight

We can, we will, we are shutting down Satan dieconomie daily. We can because we have the ability, the knowledge and the strength. We will because our will embedded in us to this from the good Lord because we are seeing the numbers drop daily on unnecessary killings that is the power of we can, we will, we are, we need to make a billboard and put them throughout the country, all over the place. It is okay by me; feel free to do this.

This book has a part of the writing in it that says you know someone cares about your personal problems.

I found myself circling around the people with the books as if they were wagons to protect the people who go inside them until they get the power to defeat the dieconomie in Jesus' name as if the spirit of David is coming out of everyone who has this wisdom in their marrow.

Old news

Know Satan has built his world around the dieconomie. Now it is time to tear this house down and with the strength of one of the three little pigs or all together. If we huff and puff we can blow it down, since we have just arrived to make us feel like we are on time and in time to get rid of this invisible structure that has been standing so tall and prevalent in our earthly world.

The Lord is giving people a break before they need a break. So take advantage of it, if not for you for someone else.

To not raise a baby bully who might grow up to be a bullet bully or killer, there is a little book I have been giving away for years to new parents, titled, _A Gift for You_. It is a way to give a child a better chance of not going the wrong way in life and/or becoming a bully of any kind in life. It is still available to anyone.

The worse part of this state of thinking is the core problem that makes someone want to become a bullet bully. It is the under-developed or turned inside out unawareness that some people want to be a part of something at a place of inner confusion. That is known as a towerist in a hurry or faster so they become terrorists who create terror because of being able to become bullet bullies with their hand on a gun. They go to a level of not caring how things turn out and whether someone gets hurts outright and shows their hand, whether it is wrong, compared to the other kind of towerist that keeps in line with a hidden agenda. They do their best to not show their hand and do the damage where it can't be detected at first if it shows up most of the time. It has flaws that harm people.

Who are the towers? They are the rich and powerful who usually find a way to take or manipulate their way to the top of whatever game they are in and they take no prisoners, meaning if you can't hang you get left behind by any means necessary.

They have all kinds of lifestyles: steals from anyone like all drug dealers. The one thing they have in common is they want to get on the top of whatever they are doing whether it is so-called good or bad in a bad way like drug companies' CEO's or drug dealers on the street, Ponzi schemes, etc. They all have the one thing in common and that is greed for power and wealth. These are a part of Satan's dieconomie.

It drives the towerism in the average person who doesn't want to pay dues like people in general to want to be in control. They want to demand respect even if they don't give it. This is a true sign of being somewhat crazy. The best fortune sometimes has the biggest problems with it.

People may be out of control about this problem of wanting to be a towerist. They don't know it is pushing them to do wrong. If they can't stop themselves from going over the edge they may do something like rob or kill. At the same time they have a blindfold on their eyes. That is why this information helps to bring them back from the edge before they go over and take someone with them, in the name of Jesus.

Let's stop the killing by teaching the bullet bullies how not to be that way. Do we really campaign for the Lord as he wishes us to or are we playing the game with a good pitch in his house sometimes?

The wisdom is owned by you to
stop being used by the power of any demons

Keep it real

As we know if we can help save one that one might be the one who saves one more or a million.

This book is a way to help stop killing anyone, anytime, anyplace and for any reason.

God's therapy

Talking it out can be another way to help because we are to protect the children. Every time you feel vulnerable to commit an act of violence and want to harm someone, ask the Lord to bring the loveoutame and also ask him to bring the part of himself out of you. Say this as many times as you like. It will present a new you to you about the right way you need to feel about life and others and it is really a good way.

This starts with you just stopping and saying it is going to be okay. That can be the way to stop your pain and start the healing of a blister that the Lord wants you to live with, believe me. Somewhat like Paul, I know I have one and it is still with me because someone did my mother wrong and I had to do the same thing I am asking you to do. Stop and not become a bullet bully. There were a flue times or more about different things I had to ask the Lord to keep me safe from myself.

Putting out the trash

These actions of negativity can also be developed from the television and radio suggestions of violence. They sometimes trigger a response to be a bully along with violence if it is at home, verbally, mentally or physically even emotionally. It pushes a child to the edge and they push back in ways so they will not go over an edge and do some of the unfortunate things some do. Let the child know it is only television, not real life. Try to keep it separate from what you can't do in life.

This is why we need to help ourselves if you have an offspring or are a guardian to a young child growing. That way the problems are headed off thanks to the wisdom of spiritual skill development.

Learn from whomever needs to
bless yourself out of this kind of mess

To help stop a problem that may need heading off, we have enough of a workout in our lives. To do that deals with healthcare and now the unseen kind of healthcare. That makes evil come out in us as humans can end and/or stop anyone that would think of becoming a kind of zero to change. If not for anyone else do it for yourself to be a hero and to stop the bullying of any kind.

What may cause the kid of all ages to become a bully? Information that needs to be cut off so they won't grow up to be bullies. The therapy of knowing can help some by just having it out there. So speak on this every time you think it is needed and know. _Little Mr. Fix-A-Thought_ is a friend in a book I wrote that I have to share with children and adults. It gives them a good examples of how to make good choices and to respect people and not harm them.

The being stuck no more avenue

What can be said about this level of negativity is it is another part of the madness that became a part of the existence when the tower effect of wanting to be a part of something that grow tall as the Tower of Babel. But it fell or was taken down and some do not get a change to claim up on something high.

Getting back to the point. When the tower came down people fell into a confusion with the inability to communicate that helped to create the process of no unity and foolishness from failing. All Satan could do is step in to harm people he did at this time and it still exists, the taking, robbing and the list goes on, because that is what happen. Before the fall the people were on one accord.

Another step forward to like about you

If you want to know about this read the books. If we had enough people in unity could we re-unify again as we were when we started to build the tower? We wanted to see and get to heaven but without the towerist sickness that came into our lives by way of Satan when he fell at the hand of the Lord. He took advantage of us when the Lord took down the tower we were building. Think of what this would be like with an "all in for this love in us" affair. Can this be a part of the Lord's plan for us that is now being revealed?

The falling down of the twin towers is a part of Satan's destruction and death pathways. The terrorist uses this to harm Americans. But we rebuild now after all of this do we start a new building state of our spirit yes we do. We are a part of one of mankind's latest and greatest gifts made new.

A wake up call

All of the strategies have not been worked out yet, and especially on how to be best effective in the promotion to stop the bullet bullies and prevent bullet bullies from growing up in your household by heading off the problem along with stopping the killing that can go to the level of stopping it as a child and preventing it as a teen or an adult. So can we rely on the word of mouth? They say it is best to get news out.

The important thing to know is hope is there to help make us aware that we can stop lots of harm and death in America. We can help with also others who have ideas of how to eliminate this problem from our landscape. That is why we have to take it on from A to Z as we are taking the challenge to end its aggression in the world also.

Do you know the truth when you hear it?

To get down to the core of this problem of all aggression, if we look back in time at the fall of the towers of Babel, it created a fall of mankind in a way that has had recurring effects of all kinds on all levels.

Can we use this as a sign to pray for the return of this kind of unity without the building of a symbol of any kind and use a kind of hologram? That is right, a three-dimensional image formed by a light source in our minds and hearts. Let it reflect the coming together in worship and praise for the Lord on one accord as was when the Lord enjoyed us at different times in history. So let's think about how He had to stop the one idea that we can now get right in his sight. Or will you write this off as a coincidence? I pray you don't.

This is just another part of the Body of Christ that needs to be worked on and that we can share. So be one of many who will sit on the front row when called on to help.

Some might say when you're going through this kind of process of growth, it is somewhat of a spiritual metamorphosis. It is redefining the structure of the spiritual DNA to a level of newness where there is such thing as learning from a writing of the concept on how to become much more intelligent. As it is said, we only use a certain portion of our brain and our intelligence. This will put us on another level of an even more peaceful use of a greater and newer part of the intellect or the spiritual reality that works within.

Then to become a part of the healthcare industry that is needed and the first place it should be used. The best spiritual healthcare is for those who are supposed to be running the country that desperately needs to be repaired.

It is time to learn to be comfortable and fill safe in your own skin.

A note I want to share

I have been planning a hologram of a house of God in the sky for many years. It may be closer today than ever before.

As I said, the people wanted to go to heaven but don't want to pay dues. Now does this make it easier? I think so.

The biggest plus to security is
to stop this problem on all levels.

This is a part of the work of God that teaches about the key to not being a killer. It also helps parents to prevent raising a killer, thanks to God.

Being prepared for the hiccups of growth on a spiritual level that the skills give is normal.

For anyone who wants to know especially what a hooded saint disciple is you can. It is explained in the book #Enough. It also teaches teens not to harm other students in school by not becoming a bullet bully or any other kind of bully.

The Lord gave us a way to end all of the raising of bullies, stopping the bullet bullies and stopping the bullet bully killers who need to know freedom from Satan's traps.

Use your foresight

This comes from old school that wants you to think about putting some old spice thinking in your life.

This may be one of the best ways to jump the broom into the Body of Christ.

This gives hope through the presence of action to put the statements out there to be seen and understood. This way the people know that prayers have been, and are being, answered.

All day long this is the show beats tell movement of love in action. Seeing is believing. The way out of darkness can get people out of their own way. Others who need help with being or becoming a bullet bully can start the process of stopping a bullet bully sin- drome using this therapy of learning about God's wisdom.

This can work for some on an uncommon level by them just knowing that the power of love has been brought forward out of the heavenly Body of Christ. It is a fact that is real just to know you can get help sometime for some people. It is enough to stop some people from doing wrong. They just need to see some effort pointing in the right direction and this is more than a home run for that reason.

Therefore, I believe, to a certain degree, that bullying is born in some people. Having this instinct can come to some inherently but it may also be egged on by the environment they come up in. So we can teach them love is the most important project to have going on at home. However, some parents teach a different kind of love that makes them act out backward with bullying. It is a kind of an over-aggressive love that pushes people to the edge in ways where a child will act out of the ordinary. This needs to be toned down.

It may be called the take no stuff sin-drome that corrupts the child's actions and the bullying activity kicks in and takes over. This is not a for sure diagnosis but it is a start to work from. Now put your opinion in and maybe we will have it figured out.

What do we do to prevent a child from getting the bullying sin-drome? Talk to them and let them know the difference between self-protection and over-protection. Teach them to not be a bully so they will not have to pay a price later to a hellish cause.

To help some people who don't want to change because of being so-called desperate for money, please get a copy of _How to Live with Less and Gain More_. It will help end that problem. Also learn to do more for yourself with the book _Time to Stop Living on the Edge_. It is somewhat of a natural occurrence to want to be that way in life, just existing. It started from the towers of Babel then it became somewhat a part of the DNA of the human growth patterns to want to have more than they have a right to, in the wrong ways.

This is somewhat the makeup of all people but people who may have been born with an extra way of protecting themselves from this can have something I don't know about. I didn't have it and had to work my way out of the towerism I had and even when to the presence of not being responsible and wanting some kind of golden staircase to walk down out of the tower but it didn't happen because I fell on my butt and I thank God I got out without getting killed or killing someone.

#Enough is about mature reading

If someone can think of harming another person they are not too young to read this book.

I have done my homework

Born c. 460 BCE, island of Cos, Grace – died c. 375 BCE Larissa Thessaly. Regarded as the father of medicine. The facts can be one way or the other I may have been given by the Lord a healing process of spiritual medicine to help the people or I am a phony. It is not enough time to debate. I have done my homework regarding the process of spiritual skills growth to get free stay free from Satan's traps.

This can be known as a book titled *A Kaleidoscope of Knowledge*, to stop the raising of bully and the stopping of a bullet bully from killing on all levels. Now you can help yourself with all the tools that come with the blueprints to keep the blood blue.

If anyone wants to stop being any kind of bully and also become a hooded saint disciple, you should get the bigger book #Enough.

How about this for keeping it simple because that is how the Lord likes it done. It also makes it easier for some people to change that thought it would be heard.

Big news

One of the things I hope we can decrease most of all is the people who can be prevented. This will help protect the people from themselves and from going to a death row jail cell. The more we help stop the beginning of a bullet bully lifestyle the more love is known.

This requires faith. It is a way to stop killing anyone, anytime, anyplace and for any reason. All you have to do is cross the T's and dot the I's.

People need to take the reasoning power of self-love and apply it to someone they are at odds with and see hatred disappear.

This process of thinking on a therapeutic level is a process of someone having to get themselves a demonectomy. It is a way to put a part of one's self outside or inside of themselves to cover the outside of their actions. Now it may be somewhat whacky sounding but it works.

Because of student activity we don't want to be confronted with a level of getting too new or too quiet so this is persecution message. This is done because if the spiritual maturity has not had a real excuse, it can be like a nuclear relaxer to help the spirit get used to the strengthening process.

Proverb: the father who ate sour grapes
Ezekiel 18:1-3
1. The word of the Lord came to me again, saying, what do you mean when you use the proverb concerning the land of Israel, saying,
2. What do you mean when you use this proverb concerning the land of Israel, saying: 'the fathers have eaten sour grapes, and the children's teeth are set on edge?
3. "As I live," says the Lord God, "you shall no longer use this proverb in Israel.

I am a member of the anti-bullet bullying club to help stop the child from going into a development that causes them problems, from not growing up right, that may cause them to be de-sensitized to others' feelings and that is not healthy for anyone.

A new level of love has come forth to increase the power that mankind is in need of. One reason I do this is when I was a young student, I couldn't get along with bullies and I couldn't get along with myself.

Adults

Quit bragging on weapons to kids: it is an opening. This stops kids from killing kids. It has gotten that bad for Satan to teach a kid to want to hurt others and they have a natural gravitation to negativity as a bully. This is the true reverie of life to win the process of growing. The principles people use, I use the book *Little Mr. Fix-A-Thought* to help children make good choices in life.

Synopsis for big book

This book starts out to help stop school killing but it broke off as a way to end all kinds of patterns of harm. It has the tools of wisdom that can help someone stop themselves who want to harm others. It has been written for mature teens and adults.

It talks about spirituality on a growth level that doesn't include religion of any kind. The other books also help end the presence of Satan and decreasing his dieconomie of death that can stop from decreasing the presence of its working to see the loveoutame that stops the plans that Satan has in order to increase the Body of Christ with human salvation.

If anyone is overly concerned about the way the country is going, you can gain a peace of mind by reading a book *Calm During the Storm*.

To get off of that kind of mountain I suggest you read the one book but also read *Fixing What is Broken in America by Stopping Towerism*, then *All Peoples Handbook*, to get some sky under your belt. It is a way to go that you should know. This is a part of the first stand to become a noble spirit and soul owner. So let's get started with all that we got.

Pain can stop in certain ways

It hurts my heart to say that Satan's dieconomie has crossed over borders and covered all areas of life, where no set of laws can be free from weathering the ungodly wrath of Satan. It has pitted family against family and left out no people who are committing crimes against others.

Rainbow time for all

Congratulations for being a part of this. It may be one of the first times ever that mankind has been given the ability to throw water on Satan in a spiritual way. If the vision of the Wizard of Oz adventure can melt a wicked spirit with a bucket of water then we as a nation of people can dump buckets of water on ourselves to make a point and show some love. Why can't we at least try to end a dieconomie and rain on this parade of death from foolishness? To learn to tell the truth.

The sky chief disciples and the hooded saint disciples work together

Does the whole world need to take a time out to put a stop to the dieconomie so no one else gets used by Satan to do his bidding? We are an intelligent people but we have let ourselves become hornswoggled and put in a or be stuck in a blindsided position that we can get out of thanks to the will power we were endowed with by God.

Human nature is an uncontrollable power that sometimes youth, especially pre-teens and early developing youth have that gets out of control and causes them to act out and become radical toward others. It can be controlled. It is just like the development of anything that needs guidance. It requires a little time effort by the parent/guardian at first then it can be matured into the right frame of development. You just have to work at it.

We are supposed to learn from the lessons in life. Can we take on of the biggest lessons from one of the major blunders created by mankind? Turn it around and take all knowledge we can out of it to create a new kind of justice and that is learning from what took place at and because of the tower of Babel and its coming down. What problems occurred behind it and where can we go from now after all of this time? We can learn about the other destruction it created in order to reconstruct at least the nature of man coming together again in a soulful way. It can also provide a better kind of harmony from all of the lessons we've learned that created towerism, the dieconomie and the individuals who want to kill and destroy. Can we turn all of this around from this one major lesson? It has now been disclosed to us and de-cloaked to us.

That is right the loveoutame flower that has been around forever. Now it is time to be recognized that it comes out of us and blossoms, blooms and has a sweet fragrance to it. We can use the oils that come out of the process to develop even more grace and glorify the Lord in great ways with the help of this teaching.

It is time to welcome all of the next generations and inform them about the loveoutame flower that is within that cannot be dominated by any of Satan's dieconomie.

They say if we raise a child right and they go astray they will come back. If we raise a child on the principles of how to stay away from the dieconomie and they do go astray at least while they are out there they will not create a hellish situation.

They say that sometimes the best is saved for last. Maybe this is saved for last for mankind to find a new level of greatness within themselves.

The Lord is tired of us punishing ourselves to hell. I guess this is coming from me. I thought we would figure out the reason why before now. I guess that is why he chose me because I was a willing vessel to take whatever confrontation that could come from me telling this truth about the foolishness of us in not using the blessings and understanding and wisdom we have been given. I am not special just a willing vessel. I intend to stand up for the Lord and tell what he wants to be understood about what Satan has put on so many in his dieconomie of death.

Do not be a wicked, unlawful or slothful person.
Proverbs 18:9
9. he who is slothful in his work is a brother to him who is a great destroyer.

Could we say that the Lord is going to war now? Yes and he is equipping the multitudes with enough to defeat Satan.

The Lord is deputizing now. Become a soldier in his army. With this knowledge you are equipped. Tell it, tell it all!

Getting away from under the curse of Nero, if you don't know who he is it is time to learn. I will let you know he had towerism and was a big part of Satan's diecomnome as well as a sick man.

It is a great time to start witnessing to yourself. The one thing that you will not do is fulfill your gift if you are not saved. You have to be saved first and get your salvation before you receive your gift because anyone can claim they have one.

This is one of God's laws not mans. So if you are not really saved you will not be able to manifest your gift. That is a harsh but real fact.

If these books can help stop and deter one person from killing another person it will be looked at as it should be as another level of the Lord's love that he has blessed us with. He feels we are worthy. Do we need to make ourselves worthy by becoming learned about this and his word more daily?

We are de-cloaking the end of the invisible bully. It appears in the present state of thought that was once not even examined within the facts of knowing who it was. Satan is who he is and now that we are aware, we can see him just as plain as day, in a kind of silhouette of darkness that is the real deal invisible bully. He is the culprit of all the activity that tries to steal, kill, and destroy humans in the earthly realm. Once we are with the Lord in the spiritual realm, he no longer can succeed in anyway harming us and or causing us to harm each other. So we strive for that freedom that is our will that creates our perfection in the complete reality that we live in. That is there thanks to God, Amen.

Satan bullies people who are not wise enough to stop him with the power of the Lord. He causes them, in more than one way, to do things they don't really want to do and/or he makes them think it is their idea.

What is one of the worst things people do? They act complacent about life's trials and tribulations that comes people's way. People need to wake up and not let themselves be put in this blue state of life. This can be done by knowing the good news to be used.

What can this all mean? It is time to give up and stop fighting with yourself so you can come out of the jail on the inside of you that your past put you in. What you think makes a difference and matters.

Wellness comes with enough. I hope this is enough to do more than enough good in your life. I also hope you have enough to share with others so they too get enough. The Lord supplies more than enough for everyone. It is time to put on your armor.

Sometimes people are vulnerable enough to believe the truth and at other times they are not. What time is it for you?

Therapy

The blind can see once you begin to understand this eye opener that the Lord gives and no one else including Satan can take it away. It can be placed in the 3rd or 4th place of love: 1. Agape; 2. Eros; 3. Philia; and 4. loveoutame. I am thankful to my Lord that he has fulfilled the cries and dried up the tears in my eyes.

A profound truth

The best way to win a war is to be prepared for it. So it is time to get to know your true enemy. If you want to get ahead this is how to keep your enemy close to you. To win it over by the way of do what the Lord said. Do your homework. If it was all given to you it wouldn't be worth it. I will tell you once you win the enemy over give the glory to God because he is the one who teaches us all.

Ephesians 3:14-15
14. For this reason I bow my knees to the Father of our Lord Jesus Christ,
15. From whom the whole family in heaven and earth is named

Psalms 48:14
14. For this is God, our God forever and ever; he will be our guide even to death.

God's direction is always the best. He will be our guide. He is there to help you through the road-blocks, detours and speed bumps that discourage us. That is why Jesus uses his cross, his work and his people to motivate us on the journey to keep us following him and staying focused.

Welcome to the get fixed and get fit squad

Stop if you have a gun and think it gives you power to teach someone how tough you are then you may be a bullet bully. The fact that if you think you will commit a crime of any kind with it, then you might be a bullet bully. Who is the foot soldier leader of bullet bullies? It is Satan and you can free yourself from that bondage. If you don't know you are most likely to kill or murder or vice versa.

Satan took the one foundational principle and multiplied it and monopolized it to the max to get as much death and destruction out of it as could be and he is still doing it. The downfall of the tower of Babel. The books can tell you more.

If You have been hooked up by the towerism affect to a level of patterning the fall and you can understand the principles of the ways the prince of darkness set up people to do his bidding to help them pay their own way into hell. It is like the Lord pays your way to heaven but Satan has set up his trickeries to make people pay their way into hell because he can't do it for you. But as a master of disguise he can show you how you can do it for yourself. That is all he has to do all the time.

Now if you don't think he is not smarter than some people then why is there so much wrong done and harm to people. It is because they know not what they do at first and forget or are blind to the consequences at the time of darkness. So let's teach as many as we can to know Satan's set up so they won't be let down into the ground to not come up again property.

The mouth of teeth only want you to stand up and act grown not like a goat with a headache. It is the best time in life to not be one who wants someone else to be or feel like they are responsible for you. It is time to be your own person and not have guilt about your life because you the right things.

It is a blessed and festive time for learning to be free of this curse for all who may fall into Satan's dieconomie. You can now be awakened and made aware that no harm can come to you.

If you add more to your life

To be known by the things you are doing with Bound to Heaven Publishing/Ministries becoming a custodian of the world.

The downfall of an era

Even Satan knows we are not perfect. He uses the dieconomie principles to cause the presence of stealing, killing and/or destroying any way he can.

This was his biggest stronghold on mankind that has been taken away from him in a mighty way.

It is time we raise each other up to a heavenly place on earth higher than Satan can approach with his dieconomie. We are in charge of raising ourselves up. Additionally, we are not to depend on the Lord for certain things until we earn them.

The son or sun roof top is open

Satan made the best out of the killing deal of humans making mistakes killing on all levels. He is getting as many people as he could to die before they are saved by accepting Jesus as Lord and Savior.

There are many kinds of ways that a bullet bully kills people. I think the worse way is when the innocent get killed, a child foremost. This destroys the very fiber of a family from the inside out.

It is such a darn shame that most bullet bullies can't even shoot straight. They are blindly firing a gun. Only God knows what their punishment is going to be. To have to live with an inner hell once inside can't be something anyone really wants. So get with the anti-dieconomie program to help stop the wildness and letting Satan control you. The dieconomie has had so many ways it works to harm people. It is time to keep the blood blue.

We the people have to put ourselves in a position to keep life sacred and as free from Satan's level of darkness. That is why it is now so needed to warn the world of the ways of desperately. Satan has devised to murder, kill and harm people using people.

That is why we are the keepers of the blue blood. To stop it from turning red as much as we can gives us the position of hooded saint disciples. We can also stop Satan from harming anyone we can before they have a chance to receive the Lord in their life. It is like a crown of joy we wear and share with the Lord.

This is the part when the Lord shows you how to take back your heart from Satan. If you never took ownership to it, it has been free for the taking. How many people have ended up with broken hearts because they never took ownership? How many has Satan taken over causing them to destroy their life by suicide? He causes some, and I was one, to not want to live. I got a way out like you are getting.

It is ownership time. That way we are cleaning house and opening up to know that the spirit on the inside of some of us at one time or another has been lonely and Satan knowing this. His plan is to give it enough attention to not be to notice and take over the state of someone's actions. Add to that a kind of death wish for some in any way he can get it. That is why we have to feed the spirit as if we are starving with this wisdom so it knows the right things to do and not get put in one of Satan's trick bag.

All I can say is welcome back home if you went away went astray or did some kind of dirt yesterday. Again, welcome back and what may be strange is some people didn't know in a sense of speaking they were gone because they never knew they were at home.

All can consider this a holistic renewal development of life. It gives a brand new way to think of your life in the first place. It also gives a new key to start it all over again with more tools in the way of spiritual skills to get less resistance in the daily development of your earthly journey.

Here we go again

The new day is dawning and the sun is going to be bright. The undercover bad, being a devil, has come out of the shadows and the loveoutame flowers are growing and seemingly good. I say hallelujah for just this reason alone.

The bottom line is anyone who has to prove they are a man (or woman) by becoming a bullet bully is nothing but a bullet bully chump. There is nothing thorough if you have to have the devil do the fighting for you. That is all there is. If you are a man you behave like a man and not like a bullet bully chump. If your brain can't work it out get a court of law.

It is time to learn how to not be a bullet bully. A man who cannot work within a diplomatic arena isn't worth the time to talk to.

There are studies that state that we are declining in our IQ scores. It has been happening over the last four decades. There are many reasons for this but the thing we must learn most from it is we can increase it now in another state of growth on a spiritual skills basis.

If you know someone who is thinking they are making the right choices but don't know themselves, do you think you can trust them? This includes you.

It is wonderful thing getting to know you and getting to know all about you without fear of choices and decisions.

Now is the time when you can escape from wrong decision making to do the right things to earn the trust you need to have in order to succeed. Put your mind in the right place and begin to develop the understanding to bring about the right choices for your chances to continue to grow in life. Learning spiritual skills is the best thing you can do for yourself.

Why should I be afraid of someone who is afraid of me? If I am afraid of me then who else am I afraid of? The other side of the coin is if I don't know I am afraid of me then where am I in the equation? That may mean I am confused, misguided, not able to be trusted, waiting to be busted and the list goes on. In order to get off that list of being a fool, somewhat crazy or mentally deranged. I need to know me so I can be outside of the numb-dumb void-noid lame-duck issues.

Some would say it is time to step up to reality and stop faking the reality that you don't understand.

When people don't know themselves they could be a traitor, a terrorists, a terror or an individual who harms themselves or others because of fear of themselves and others. It is time to get out of the melting pot that leads to hell.

Know this, help yourself because no one can help you more than you can. If you are depending on someone else to do it for you, you will be stuck like chuck on first base, if you even make it there.

Get some real drive to stay alive

If you don't get any drive to stay alive, don't go around with your head hanging down and blame everyone else for your problems that you may be afraid to escape and free yourself from. That is what usually happens, blaming someone who doesn't have anything to do with it, it is yours. You need to own it and confront it so you can create success and stop being the less, thinking you are the best and will be blessed.

You may need to realize that you are a part of the shiggidy crew who belongs in a zoo because you are capable of going ziggidy boo and don't know reality. If this is the case, change it.

Lose that touch of existence. Lose those moments of non-reality where you can get caught up in the boo crew to scare the hell out of yourself in your mind and bring it to the table to someone who doesn't have anything to do with it, including family, friends or whomever.

We must come to the conclusion that once someone starts putting substance in their bodies, it can become one of the biggest crutches there is in making someone continue to run away from themselves and fear who they are. It can have a double, triple and sometimes quadruple blockage to getting through to who you are. If that be the case you may need outside help and that is something you will be responsible for seeking, getting and maintaining. As it is said, you can't through to yourself until you know yourself. You might say that is just another part of the getting to know you process of reality.

If you think of it, it may be a blessing in disguise to have a substance that pacifies you so you can get along with yourself since you fear yourself. Once you get rid of it you know there is greater room for growth.

Abusing power is something towerists are known for. That is one thing we need to stay away from? The abuse of power is like having a weapon in your hand. Abusing someone with it by bullying people with it is like being on the lower level of towerism. It is just as dangerous and crazy as being on a higher level of towerism. It is a level of negativity that you can be released from if you are aware that it exists. So bully towerism vortex freedom is what it is all about.

In other words, freedom from being sucked in to become a sucker of Satan of some kind is what we are not going to allow to happen to us in this life.

I may stand corrected, freedom to not get sucked into the vortex of towerism and becoming a bully and more so a bullet bully.

The process of being at war with one's self and even to a negative level of being in a spiritual war with one's self where the good collides with the bad. Not knowing these things exist of course gives negative satanic powers to rule over one's self. To become aware and being made known gives light to freedom to have no negativity flowing out of you but having positive energy flowing out of and through you.

Now is the time to prevent Satan from having that influence over your existence in ways that create detrimental situations. No one is perfect but no one has to create a detrimental existence for anyone else. Such as when you go to be a bullet bully you may run into someone who is there to stop the bullet bully or someone who is a bigger bullet bully than you.

The bullet bully is usually doing something wrong. Now you can gain freedom that is necessary to be blessed and not cursed.

Taking it to the furthest aspects of understanding, the worse towerist is one who is an ordained towerist or someone who stands in the clergy and is all to themselves. Next is one who feels they have a calling for the Lord as a towerist to so-called project a reality that belongs to some kind of demonic presence that they are not aware exists in them. That is why they say that those who sit in towers of darkness and high places are to be de-throned by the presence of goodness when they are confronted.

We have to be prepared to de-throne those who sit in towers of darkness in our presence. Let them know, whoever they are or whatever think they are about and how they think they are supposed to be doesn't work like that in the kingdom of God's presence. His building and his trees that he has planted are grown to be known as the fruit of the earth. Amen

To be able to express this and have the knowledge of teaching this requires you to be prepared for the unexpected. It will confront you in a way to make itself feel comfortable because you are going to make it uncomfortable. You won't care because you have put on your armor and have all your garments to cover you. You do not have to worry about the darts and arrows that try to defeat you but they will not. You are in the fight to make sure everything stays right.

There are even some individuals who, through the use of drugs, try to put themselves under a trance or some kind of spell thinking they are greater than others. They have themselves in a lost dimension in claiming victory over the fact of being lost without any knowledge or conception that they are one of those in a void-noid numb-dumb sin-drome process of development. They may be locked in a toweristic level of thinking, acting and sharing what they think is greatness that is really not as great as they think. We don't have to figure them out they have to figure themselves out and that is hard to do.

Stay away from those things that Satan has hidden in you to cause you to think on that level. The downfall of the tower of Babel would cause all of these chain reactions of negativity. Once we captivate these understanding and put it in its place we can create more freedom throughout the world.

Wherever I mentioned the pope is on dope you really need to say the pope is on dope and dopemines which is a natural kind of high, they really need to watch themselves. But they are human also. The pope got on the dope this past year when he dealt with a situation when you cracked his bulb and started talking outlandish and out of character. That is what I mean about the pope on dope.

I must now thank the Lord because I have become de-ghettorized. In other words the ghettoism of satanic relationships of existence that don't produce fruit are no longer a part of my development. De-ghettoized so I can realize the full potential.

It is time that we learn that every dimension of criminal activity has been enhanced by the bullying process and theory. It is a part of the redevelopment of principles of the fall of the Tower of Babel being enhanced. It had a put in place because of the fall and the confusion of not being able to communicate and still wanting to reach for something higher than we should want to reach for in life or reality. Therefore, criminal activity has been enhanced. However, it can be denounced also in the process so that we can develop a more unified positive imagery for ourselves as humans in the eyes of the Creator.

41

This is why this knowledge has always been there but has now come to the forefront in being released daily to stop the actions of negativity that deal with crime. Crime basically is a development of sin. So free yourself from these elements of ungodly processes of wanting to change a part of reality that is not for the right reasons and get on a pathway to change this reality for the sake of humanity. In Jesus' name, Amen

To get things in the proper perspective, the spiritual warfare that we are in within ourselves adds to the dieconomie especially throughout the years. Law enforcement has had a presence of negative sides of dislike, hatred and ungodliness causing a lot of lives to be taken by Satan's dieconomie. This occurred through the law enforcement process that we are now trying to fix, at least in America. Hopefully it will catch on throughout the world, this policy of understanding a parliamentary procedure of love which is greater than hate if we let it manifest in the way that it should so we all can be blessed by it.

There is too much prejudice but the main thing is there is too much demonology where people idolize the demon process of thinking and adapt them to the relationship with themselves. They portray these things to others causing them to stay in the place of confusion leaving them in the numb-dumb void-noid sin-drome process.

It all leads back to one thing and that is finding a way to create harm, hurt and pain and eventually leads to Satan's dieconomie.

We can be delivered and understand the power of knowing "no" to deny us from becoming a bully, a hood rat, or any kind of individuals who uses a weapon to be a bully for the sake of their own gratitude or for the sake of the dollar. It weakens them because they don't have the ability to give up the dollar. It weakens them because they want to be in the blind state of existence.

I had to deny myself I had to turn down from being a bullet bully and maintain this for all of the rest of my life once I had that challenge in my life. As a matter of fact, I never used a weapon to be a bullet bully even though the thought came into my mind several times throughout the years when I was young. Once I became older it never dissipated into a thought process of mine.

Learning to not become a child bully is necessary. We do this by teaching the youth to learn how to not become a bullet bully. They can learn not to be a killer and they won't let Satan steal their life from them.

This process of learning is like preparing, treating and mending a wound that has a need for adjustment before it can be worked on or needs to be taken care of until it is ready and healing or renewal is happening. This knowledge is the bandage and it is all you need in God's name so use it.

This process of healing is like being under God's insurance plan. It is free you only need to get the knowledge wherever you are broken. The repairs will be made with the knowledge that Dr. God supplies.

This process of help is like being on the battlefield without any armor or are not prepared for incidents such as the fact that we all have been wounded. That came from birth but God has multiplied his love. He is looking for those who want to be survivors to pick them up to fix them in mind body and soul. Amen

This process of negativity that may enter into someone's life is like growing up without a parent around to teach them the right things to do to prepare them for being out in the world. A protection plan with your guardian, the Lord, is now seeing the emergency situation. It is sending the information that is needed about safety and love that you were not given before, or taught that it was available in this manner.

This is a downfall to stay away from

There are some people who get under the influence of a substance. Their brain realigns because it becomes discombobulated. That is why you must be careful of what goes into you.

There are people out there who I have heard about that have killed and didn't mean to, whether it was a best friend or a family member. The fact of the matter is, once it happened there was nothing to be done. The process of trying to be healed is something that no one needs to live with. To take a loved one away is a big void that will be in someone's life about this. It is time for the 411 and the 911 so it can become a whole healthy person and not a person who is living in darkness to cause harm to self or others.

This process is like being under
the covenant or covering of the Lord

I can't explain why one book has to be divided into three. I guess one is for the Father and one for the Son and the Holy Spirit.

Add to sight

The situation of being vulnerable is not healthy. We are like a bunch of people who are in a play. Every time we are in need of assistance, the Lord dispatches angels to look over us. Sometimes if we are not fully protected it is because we have been disobedient and not didn't listen to the word of God. In this play we want to make sure we have the angels to cover us and Satan to pass us by. This is something we look forward to, the devil passing us by, due to the angels who are watching over us to protect us.

Therapy

What is God's insurance? It is the added love that he supplies to anyone who opens the door and lets him in to bring his message to you. You do not have to go far. You can receive it right where you are.

The real rewards in life come from being a part of the true Body of Christ. Believe it, there is a fake part of the Body of Christ that Satan controls. Now you should be able to manage your understanding with

God's wisdom and not be a part of what Satan rules over.

More about author

When we get down to the bare knuckles of what I am talking about, as far as being a bullet bully, I have never totally been a bullet bully. I have known them and somewhat associated myself with them. I have been one who was, in my younger days, an armor bearer.

The fact of the matter is, I have been tempted but never fulfilled that label. You could say I have been around individuals who have done things that has made me uncomfortable so I backed out of that process of growth. I had the motivation of my parents who kept me spiritually enlightened and grounded because we were a God serving church family, even though we had issues.

At the same time you could say I was not a pistolero but a pistol-ferrow. I had to be an armor bearer to protect myself from others who wanted to try me or basically take what I had. It was about self-preservation in my level of growth.

At one time I sold marijuana. It was a lucrative trade and hustle along with other substances. I was introduced to it by family members and they were in the trade so it kept me where I had to know how to protect myself. I never was involved with using a weapon to take or harm others because of some foolish or crazy action of wanting to become a towerist to be noticed or someone who felt they were powerful over others. I didn't get into that because I had a spiritual reality that I was motivated to keep in touch with. It granted me spiritual skills along with the fervent prayers of my parents and grandparents which kept me blessed to do what I am doing which is teaching others that they can be someone who is not a bullet bandit or bully bullet bandit.

The one time I think I would have taken a shot at someone (and I wasn't the only one) was when a murderer/rapist killed women in my neighborhood. One of the women was my friend's mother.

I have seen people rob and kill. I have seen people retaliated on, killed and shot before my eyes. I have even had to put my finger on someone's gut to stop the blood from squirting out. There have been many dimensions of finding out the effects of bullets from finding out someone's life had ended to destroying someone's love. It has brought about so much change and pain.

As I came up I lost quite a few friends who died because of the bullet bully war sin-drome that it has rocked my soul to the bottom of my eternal being. I know that it is something that Satan has put out and we are confronted with it every day but have no knowledge or power over it. That has changed and now we can utilize the power and strength to understand the loveoutame flower that can cure this sickness, madness, curse and disease.

I can help!

I have shot up a club at a time when I was conned out of some money. I did not feel good after I did that. No one got hurt but I made up my mind I would not put myself in that kind of position again, that is the bottom line. We do not have to put ourselves in the wrong situations if we think of the consequences.

I have dad to draw down on a group of four. I had to warn them to stay out of trouble because if they got caught doing wrong, they may meet a fate that might not be healthy. I did this because one of my younger brothers had been jumped earlier that day by four guys. I was unable to totally identify them so I let them go unharmed. I know the sense of it came upon me. What would I have done if they were the ones.

There have been other times when I came close to going all the way to becoming a bullet bully. Thank God I never did. Even while dealing with the situation of the rapist/murderer I showed restraint. Since it was what we would call my collar, I had the say so on both of the culprit's lives.

I am not proud of having been a young man who was locked down in four different institutions. However, I never got a charge for a weapon (being a bullet bully).

I do not want to elaborate on some of the things I have talked about. In this book I want to get down to the concept of how to end the process of the bullet bully sin-drome.

To make things perfectly clear about this scenario, I thank God that by his grace and mercy I was not one who fell under the pistol bandit sin-drome to want to take or steal from, or harm others, even though I possibly ran with those who did in my youth. I am thankful that I had that covering on me, even though there were other places in reality where I didn't understand I had covering on me but I am thankful for what I had in Jesus name. It is not bragging it is notifying anyone who wants the understanding that I was free from falling all the way into that darkness.

I know one person who was a friend of mine. He killed a pharmacist on Lee/Harvard back in the day. He was not even that kind of person but due to the circumstances of his upbringing he fell under that negative process and it cost him just about all his life in jail. Even if you don't go to jail you may go to hell. I wrote a book _Freedom from Satan's Zone_ that could save you a jail or hell sentence that deals with basically being a foolish bully (who may carry a weapon also).

There were two incidents in my life where I was going to be a bullet bully but fortunately before I arrived there they had already had expiration work done on them by other bad people or bullet bullies. Only God knows who they were. I have also reneged at two other times in committing a crime as a bullet bully thanks to the Lord and that makes about three times. The two other times were taken care of by God knows who. Really not much to talk about just a thought that reminds me that I have been there. Thank God for the spiritual skills that kept me away from crimes such as that. That is to harm someone with a weapon.

Therapy

To add this level of knowledge under your belt will give you a level of reasoning power that can grant you immunity from allowing Satan to cause you to destroy a life or a family leaving loved ones without their counterpart. This knowledge is truly a magnificent presence to have in a place within your heart. To be able to share this is like a feast where all can share in the blessings and enjoy a meal of love.

God's therapy

What can we say is the major thing that the loveoutame flower does? It eliminates, it discards and frees people from the bondage of being tormented or plagued with demonization and/or evil thoughts of a level to harm others and one's self. The loveoutame flower is like a project within one's self that is one of God's greatest tools to bring about a refreshing revitalizing way of projecting the love to self.

Self-love is one of the most important things we can possess. It can develop and fight off any satanic sickness that tries to make you not conscious of your actions when it comes down to harming others or yourself. The power of the loveoutame project transfers the love from one level to another. The transference is such a spectacular thing it is like a miracle taking place within your mental, physical and spiritual being. It is real and no one can take it from you.

Therapy

To help deactivate Satan's dieconomie use this therapy. It will work to stop you from being affected. Think of yourself as if you need to become as light as possible. The only way to do this is to detach yourself Satan's principles. Once that is done you come out of a cocoon of sort so you can fly like a butterfly, an eagle or an angel. Keep this in mind all of the time, especially when a demon of the dieconomie tries to get you to become a predator for Satan.

I don't want you to be incomplete;
I want you to be made whole

We are on our own side when we learn to lift the Lord's presence and put his name up before all mankind. We must try to take the ungodliness back to a place of its beginning, which was the Garden of Eden. We as humans can't do anything about that but wc can change the level of sin when it comes down to death. That is what we are doing to help stop as much pain as we can.

Beware

It doesn't matter who you are if you are using a weapon (or intending to use a weapon) to harm and Satan recruits you. You can use it and be wrong, such as the police in the latest killing of a young black man. Getting caught in Satan's trap is a place of darkness.

51

That is why *A Peace Offering for the Police and People* is good for the peace officers along with the other healthcare level of mental and spiritual wellness professions.

M-N

The bottom line is to not kill so you won't take a chance on getting killed in more than one way.

The forever keepsake

You can keep yourself from going temporarily insane because it can happen in the dieconomie. Afterward when you come back to your right mind it may be too late to take back what you may have done. So don't be sorry later but be aware and forewarned now to stay away from darkness. To be known by the things you are doing with Bound to Heaven Publishing/Ministries proves you are a good citizen of the world.

M-N

The main reason we don't love each other anymore is we don't know each other more, starting with self.

The power of the loveoutame transfers the love from one level to a greater level. The transformation is such a spectacular thing it is like a miracle taking place within a physical, mental and spiritual being, once you accept it and understand it is there and it is real and yours and no one can take it from you.

This is truly a blessed time. So wake up and receive your blessings in order to be free and stay out of the way of Satan's dieconomie. Never fall into this trap that creates an inevitable possibility of hell in your life forever.

If you have never been serious in your life because you are on some kind of silliness and are thinking the carefree way is the way to be, because of your nonchalant reality, then it is time you wake up before you are in a storm. The storm I am talking about is a hell storm that doesn't supply anything but fire that looks like rain but will burn you for eternity.

Wake up: no more sleeping about this because too many people are missing out on the heaven bound process of life and growth. Death is final and you need not apply early or allow Satan to put you there early. There should be no more applying for hell. Satan is taking people's applications left and right and it is time to stop.

God is recruiting and has forces beyond any measure that Satan could ever present. God is showing you more of what life is all about and the love he is offering. It is time for you to deny the one who wants to send you to oblivion and cause you more pain than you could ever imagine.

We are freeze framing the process of getting out of the grips, bondage and traps that Satan has for us. We have put a freeze on all of his measures of satanic activities that attracts us to wickedness. That is a part of our natural inclination of life. We can avoid all of this by staying focused on disallowing Satan's dieconomie to flourish.

What can be considered one of the best parts of this analogy of love and the presentation of this information of wisdom is the fact that you are slaying the dragon before you have to ride it and get burned. It is definitely a spit-fire idle presence of an image that we are not going to let affect our lives. The idle presence of an image in a dark place as a dragon that rides us into hell spitting fire all the way there is what we are not going to be a part of. This is an image of darkness that has come to light in which people are jumping on daily to ride a dragon into hell. We are not going to allow this to take place anymore because we are staying out of Satan's dieconomie.

We take the invisible concepts of darkness and bring them to light in a realistic state of mind. We can succeed in the presence of God so we can complete all of the Body of Christ and fulfill our destiny as his children. We have to collectively develop ourselves and gather our strength. Put them all into the right categories and mature ourselves so we can become a greater nation of people.

This may be the reason why he put this melting pot together so we can be the ones who lead the forefront into the heavenly body of reality and then to the heavenly body of Christ in heaven.

Are we not a part of the family of the Body of Christ? Are we not a part of the Lord's grove? The Lord has put us together to unify, teach, grow, love and even to sacrifice when necessary for other's to live in a harmonious lifestyle with peace. Therefore, if we are not fulfilling our responsibilities then we are failing the Lord and that is why we fail each other. We are supposed to fulfill each other's needs then the Lord is fulfilled. Get back on track if you have lost your reality. You are needed immediately.

To help us all on earth understand how to end this thing called the dieconomie: imagine for a minute that you are alive thousands of years ago. Everyone you turn to has no communication with family, friends, children, strangers or anyone. There is no communication at all, only babbling among one another. Close your eyes for a moment and say "Lord be it ever so humble there is no place like home." Home is where the heart is so reach back up in time and realize where we are now then see the wonders of it all and the communication that you can establish.

You can consider this the real lost that is now found

I have a thought process I am experiencing now. They say sometimes the Lord will allow his child to come home due to a specific act, even though it may be an unpleasant act. Now I am rethinking that so that maybe it is Satan's dieconomie allowing him to take something beautiful as a child away so we will miss more of the love we share with each other. Now I am caught between a rock and a hard place on this. What do you think? The other thought is the child may need to be protected before it gets any older and lost in the world. Now the Lord can take the child back home.

It is time to stop making others lame and maiming them and crippling them because you are the one who is the lame and cripple person on the inside of your spirit. Get the fixer-upper that the wisdom of the Lord has to help you get well so you can stop harming others.

Is it time to get to know who you fear to prevent the badness that could happen?

Do you want to know why so many people are attracted to guns? It is because the confusion of a curse and the forefathers gnashing their teeth. That is still going on out of fear of people even their own kids, even more so people fear themselves to a degree. You fear others if you don't know enough about yourself deep down inside and you fear yourself on a subconscious level and that needs to end.

I will say it again, it is a process of thinking on why so many people get attracted to guns. There are more than one thoughts on this. One is the fear of others and the other is the fear of self. Why do so many people get caught up on killing? I have given you one main reason in this book. I will give you more reasons in the other two books.

Why are so many more men going coo-coo cachoo and cracking their bulb? It is because they have not been taught how to stand on their own two feet. They have a sin-drome of a child who has been propped up but they fear standing on their own they need to learn more of what freedom is and know of what the gnashing of teeth means and its curse, to become an adult and that is what is up. A label of what someone is isn't what they may be.

To help with some of the reading, try meditating on the Scriptures I have told you about. To add love to this, one of the best ways to help you is in the Holy Bible. It is the number one book.

Therefore, if you fear others and if the past has the wrong kind of seeds planted in you, you are in a bondage of a kind that will hunt you and you don't know it. So if you are one who has a gun as a fool you might be a candidate to work within Satan's dieconomie. That is why you have the gift to stop him and are proud to do so. All in heaven can see God's victory in you.

One of the greatest things I can offer is help so you have a better chance of moving into the light. I hate to go through the darkness before I was able to get out of it. I feel safe now. All that is left for you is to believe that you have a way out of this kind of darkness.

Bottom line: the more you know about your enemy the weaker their defense is and the stronger you become. This is also true for the principalities of darkness by way of letting in the light.

That is why you become a fortress to a pathway of light that is created to show others how to get over, around and under the setup that has been put before mankind to lead him to a hell hole of darkness. Satan wants to welcome people to end their spiritual well-being.

Can you make the pathway out of darkness clearer for as many as you can, even to help your enemy? It is the truth of what a real disciple does. So don't fear being one. It is one of the healthiest ways to live.

We allowed a generation of foolish ignorant youth to get away from us resulting in a long line of death being left for us to see. It is time to put up a new kind of force-field to protect all humans as if it is a new kind of super hero that has been brought on earth to stop Satan's dieconomie. The dieconomie has gotten so bad it is using people to harm others with violence.

This may, in many ways, help anyone keep the blood blue and also make it even bluer daily.

The negativity of Satan is the dieconomie. Don't put this in the rear view mirror of life. It is big news to always keep in front of you.

Never egg on a person, this can even be you, who may have a dieconomie state of mind. They may be, to a degree, demonized and need to get the help, such as what you are learning in this book, to get free.

The righteous soul and spirit will be troubled about what is going on in the world. It will want to fix it. That is a part of why we are here on earth, to prove we love the Lord before we leave.

Matthew 6:3-7

3. But when you do a charitable deed, do not let your left hand know what your right hand is doing,

4. that your charitable deed may be in secret; and your Father who sees in secret will Himself reward you openly.

5. "And when you pray, you shall not be like the hypocrites. For they love to pray standing in the synagogues and on the corners of the streets, that they may be seen by men. Assuredly, I say to you, they have their reward.

6. But you, when you pray, go into your room, and when you have shut your door, pray to your Father who is in the secret place; and your Father who sees in secret will reward you openly.

7. And when you pray, do not use vain repetitions as the heathen do. For they think that they will be heard for their many words.

One way to not be a sinner is to use God's way to stopping the harming of people. It does not matter if you think they deserve to die. Do not be a part of Satan's dieconomie. Be in touch with the Lord's loveoutame protection just because you believe in it.

Have a healthy day and make it enjoyable

I do not have a bully heart. Have the children say it over and over. Tell others, "I don't have the need to disrespect anyone. I am not a bully heart person. I am a blessing and my heart was made to do the right thing."

Warring of the dieconomie
It is like hog weed; stay away from it
It can make you sick or even kill you.

Protect yourself from self if you may become a snap-fool. The way to go to block Satan is to have a heart that projects love and not hate.

This is an introduction to the loveoutame flower to end Satan's dieconomie and stop the killings by bullet bullies, no matter who it is or what it is about. Learn how to stop being a killer even if you think they deserve it. Stop the bullet bullies from killing with the loveoutame flowers. They are the manifestation of God's love that comes out of you.

M-N

This is not prophecy. It is deductive reasoning.

This evolution of thinking does not put us anywhere near the blue blooded octopus level that has three hearts and nine brains. So do not latch onto it. It is not human. This is a blank odyssey of thought to pass the time.

Can this book be like God's armor that is all over you along with his heart that is so big it seems like tens of thousands of them wanting to show you love? It is just a thought to think about, love from another mother or father for some but is not a difference in our heavenly father.

Be it known

There are wanna be towerists and terrorists who are geared or somewhat being guided toward the dieconomie. They have the sickness or a weakness to let sin control them. It can be fixed with wisdom applied to the mindset of actions to be denied.

The process of being fixed is like having had a spiritual schizophrenia that receives redemption through the acceptance of the loveoutame flower. It all can be broken down to a lower denominator that weakens the power of darkness so people can see their way out of darkness.

The therapy is the truth that sets us free to stop the madness, sadness, wickedness, horror and the lack of love. Knowing these things makes love automatically appear. It is the will of God that does that and no one can stop it. With faith you get a lot for a little.

Now I am listening to the Lord who is redeeming. I am putting together a pathway to help walk people out of the state where they may become a killer.

Book news

Taking note as the flower pollenates and get all of the buzzing around it the honey is produced. As the flowers grow, love grows.

Now it is time to get some closure for the process of outgrowing the past. This is something tangible that can be invented. If you had the possibility of being or having been a recruit of the dieconomie, then you have to take the last steps. If you are a weapon carrier or have possessed a weapon, it is time to get rid of it if it is illegal for you to have. The fact is if it has not crossed your mind how to discard the weapon, here are some ideas.

If it is a dirty weapon and a crime has been committed with it you may want to baptize it in a lake. I am not trying to get someone off of the hook if you did something wrong but I am not judging anyone. That is the Lord's job. What I am doing is showing a way to not do the deeds of the devil's dieconomie anymore in life.

I have thought about putting the weapons in a place of hiding and anonymously call 911 and tell them where the weapon can be found. But it would have to be disguised so another person could not find it.

Once you do this you are a new creature who can figure out what is next by the presence of the new state of the spirit you will start to experience. Even more so, to get free from Satan's camp or him being able to recruit you at a time that could have been perfect for you to comment death and/or harm and destruction will no longer be open to him because you will no not be a bullet bully.

The Lord has the need for you to share your love in a brand new way. The loveoutame flower state/stage has now become the loveoutayou flower. It is truly blessed and gives off a scent of love because you have become a diamond blue blood disciple; a beauty to behold.

To help you have a clear understanding of what it means to be a disciple, get a copy of _A Disciple Maker_. If you have any reservations about becoming a disciple see what the twelve were all about before they were disciples. To be known this isn't my doctrine it was given to me by the Lord to share with you.

M-N

Can this be like a color café? It can be something new to use on shirts to add in the clean look and feel.

M-N

An accidental shooting by someone who didn't have any business with a weapon in the first place is a part of Satan's dieconomie.

M-N

It is good to know you are under the development of the yesteryears of your life.

M-N

The process of thinking can be like putting up a railroad crossing sign for wrong way drivers that are coming onto the highway. You do not need a battery operated signal when you have the Lord's protection.

M-N

The book talks about the displacement of how to not kill when it comes down to it. Some police are tied into Satan's dieconomie. They need the additional help.

M-N

Harvest knowledge to keep up and not get left out of the real world.

Whatever you think about this book I hope you have enough courage to stand with us as peacemakers.

This plan can help anyone who feels a need to want to use a weapon on someone else for what may not be a good or foolish reason. This can be one of the greatest ways to teach yourself to wake up from the dark side of no self-protection.With out this wisdon life can become a nightmare or an out of control issue that falls on some people like a pile of crap.

To help block out this dark side that Satan he wants to share with you, get an understanding of what can go wrong if the devil puts in his ½ cent. It is called the dieconomie that too many people have paid an ungodly price for that they wish they never paid.

What is the main job of the dieconomie? It is to make people become out of control and try to harm someone else or more so kill them. That is right it is the worse and best it offers.

This can become a road to freedom. You have to think about what you will have to give up to get to the beginning of the end. This is done to stop Satan's plan of pulling you under or someone who should not be!

To add my personal twist to the therapy, I am revealing the one thing that gives me pleasure to pull or take the edge off of my tension, stress, anxiety or depression if any that I had in the past, along with prayer. It has been somewhat of a helper to cure all in the last 50 plus years of my life. It was first introduced to me as a child.

Ever since I have had the greatest responsibility when passing time or giving me a way to think out a problem at the same time I am doing it. The cost is very little and even in my time of pain and when I have shed tears I was steady about doing it. It is a wonder toy/joy I will never get enough of. It is a spinning top. I have had so many years of fun by myself with the different ones I have.

If you are going to get hooked on some kind of sport or hobby, you can even make a competition out of it as I once was going to do but my time got so limited. I never did besides I only needed me to be in competition.

There are so many kinds and I time how long I can make one last and how much better I get every time I work it and put my special touch on it. I am a putter good if we ever run across one another at a competition and you better believe that.

It is time to say to yourself

I believe God gave me the power to be a winner at this level of life. I am one of his favorite children.

Therefore, if you think this is some crapola, then try it before you knock it. If you want to compare this first spin to the Svengali state of Satan who will spin you out of bound, spin you out of control, and/or spin you into hell. You have no comparison to a spinning top. All it can do is flop at the end of it circling around and around until it has dismissed the state of wanting to be the wrong kind of clown in life who doesn't want others to keep a smile on their face. So smile because it is a beautiful day.

I believe with this knowledge you will have instant memory about all that you need to supply you with all of your life.

M-N

Giving notice to all who have read this scroll

You may find yourself feeling like

You are walking on streets of gold from time to time!

M-N

It is just one of my patriotic duties to love my neighbor

Exemptors are like matadors. They keep the bull-crap from causing people pain. They control it and direct it away from running in to other.

To All; If you think about killing someone

If you think you would like to see someone dead; if you want to pay someone to kill someone; if you like to pit to people at adds to fight; if you think someone should be dead; then you are a part of Satan's dieconomie and you should get out of this negative state of mind with the loveoutame. We won't forget the people who are lost and get fooled to be a fool.

Answer

What could a bullet bully be? An accident waiting to happen. A person who wants to make a name for themselves that is out of control and can't figure any other way to do so. A person who is blind to growth and think they become so high in power to create a life matter in their hand by firing a gun or is it just a foolish person who hasn't grown up enough to know the rule of life that thou shall not kill. Satan has a finger hold on them they are not aware of that creates a kind of underlying evil that loves to add to the numbers of people dying and some of them going to hell.

There are some who wonder where things went wrong about life for some who became this way. I will say it is what it is and all we can do is try to help save as many as we can with what we have and that is the love of Jesus.

To be understood

To protect yourself and family understand that it is not a stage of the dieconomie. It is a stage of the loveoutame.

M-N

To be added to *Little Mr. Fix-A-Thought* all that is needed for the steps of adding. Tell them do to others only what they want done to them. If you do something to someone that you don't want done to you, it will come back to you. It may not be in the same way but in a way you are not going to like and that is how it is in life. You can use your own scenario. Then let them know everybody is loved by someone and we all are loved by God.

Time to get a real check-up

My eyes had a problem and it needed some attention. I went to the eye doctor and got a checkup and got glasses. I sort of knew that something wasn't right my sight got worse without the glasses on as I read books, etc. I did not do a thing about it and now I pay. It is an honest mistake or a foolish one I think it is both because I did not have the self-motivation to do something about it. I paid the price of weak sight in a way.

To anyone who has thoughts of going postal about going to a job site anywhere or any kind don't think of what it is, Satan's dieconomie he wants you to become a part of. Cut ties with the evil that is trying to fester up out of you and put on a bandage of love on it to end the state of darkness and start a place of healing in your heart.

This is the help you need to get the hell-of-Cain out of you. So you don't become disabled to live life in the fullness you were meant to live in.

M-N

It is time to stop yourself from being a coward bully.

Who are the real coward bullies? Crazy bullies and lazy bullies?

A bully is someone who won't fight fair or pick on someone who may not be able to meet their challenge and not do what it takes to make things right. It is a selfish way of ending a fight that should have had some kind of diplomacy in it. Why do so many think it is okay? It is because the influence of other people who are considered to be bullies themselves on a higher level such as our government and so many nations included that go to war and bully on other countries. It is a negative force that has a way of looking correct at the same time, when it should be looked at in a different way. One battle that is controlled by Satan's dieconomie that is a kind of loophole that traps people in a kind of spiritual fight. It only wants to lead anyone even though it is necessary to protect the country and for people to protect themselves. Being a bullet bully has no excuse. It should not trap people in a kind of spiritual fight that only wants to lead anyone it can to an outlook that requires pain and a dark side of no life. It does not matter whose life it is.

There are too many people who are trying to live up to their potential but their potential is like the opposite of knowing who they are. If you know who you are in the Lord with what he has given you, you don't have to concern yourself with living up to your potential; just be what he wants you to be.

In retrospect, this is about knowing who you are and knowing who the father says you are. Once you understand those things and consistently renew your mind with them you can develop the criteria to outgrow those negative situations that you may be confronted with.

This is not pycho-babel

Not to harp on it but the dieconomie is the dark side of a blinding force in human nature. It is hidden beyond recognition by the human eye. Its presence in the invisible world has a realm of existence that can develop a process of harming people if they are not aware through a subconscious level. It uses negative energy that we must refrain from using. We must be made aware that it is a perpetrator of the inner you to want to destroy self and others. It exists and there is no way around it, but the protection that the Lord provides can eliminate the harm that it can do.

The less unpredictable you are to yourself the better off you are. Therefore, get to know you more so you will not have a scary situation take place in your life that you are not aware of. Make sure you cover your own predictabilities so you won't be a problem for yourself.

I say this because we do not need a nation to be any more divided. It is time for us to try to come back together for the world to see us. We have to get out of the trump-odyssey that makes us think we want to be great again. We should only want to stand strong enough to be a decent place again. That is good enough, nothing more or less.

I feel N=?

I feel the blessings of the Lord moving around in people to help the country stop being the land of killing and start being the land of milk and honey. It also has a new presence of not being number one in the world of single killers and become number one in stopping the killing.

Whenever you are feeling bad or negative thoughts enter your head, you know it is the hell-of-Cain in you. Once the awareness is clear to leave the sin-drome you can exit that and do something constructive, clean house, volunteer, help someone with a chore or even try to use _Mr. Fix-A-Thought_ who is a helper in a time of need.

You do not have to let the internal combustion explosion of hell fires continue to ravage your life or someone else's life. You can put them out with water to douse the flames.

We have more equipment available to be used than anything, or anyone else. If the animals can survive then we can survive to take care of them. We are supposed to look out for them instead they are doing better than we are in some ways.

This is a systematic way for anyone to stop killing. It is individualized for all people so no one will have an excuse. All you have to do is determine that you will not be a part of Satan's dieconomie. It is been made as plain and simple as the sun coming up in the morning. The therapy is there for you. It is about life and the continual pursuit to keep as many alive at least until Satan cannot harm them.

The fact that when Satan cannot harm you does not mean you will have no pain, trials and tribulations in your life. It does mean that your eternal well-being will be taken care of by the Lord. Amen

To go through the book itself. It gives you the gratification of earning your own type of spiritual coaching degree where you can coach yourself spiritually so you can overcome lots of things that may want to confront you that you are not equipped to take on. Consider yourself a spiritual coach and then develop your level of discipleship for recognition regarding the love you have for Jesus.

We are made better every time we exempt someone from pain that they could feel, especially because of us. This is one of the key ingredients for having a successful relationship with yourself. You must exempt them from pain that you may be responsible for that they really don't want and may not deserve. Remember this for your success in life: exempt people from pain. When you do that you automatically exempt yourself from pain.

How nice is it to be known as a pain exemptor. Pain exemptors have a great big smile on your face and know that you are preventing pain on yourself and others. Pain exemptors are also those who exemplifies excellence in whatever they are trying to do.

It is such a good thing to become a defender of humanity and someone who has the power and the vision to be able to see passing through darkness to not lose track of the light and the son of God and the principles that he lived and died for.

You might say that Jesus was the only one who had to go through some kind of dieconomie. It was a dieconomie to save us from Satan's dieconomie.

The best part about this learning and process of growing is you can develop an inner-dialogue with yourself and you can share with self before you express it to others. That is wonderful to be able to clear things with self, then be able to recognize that you have the ability and the responsibility to share with others. This involves developing certain principles that people may not normally be used to.

You have to be somewhat articulate in order for you to be able accept this process of thinking along with the words you may have never heard before. Just think a little outside the box and you will be fine. One day you will be able to use them just like other words used today.

Once you learn how to articulate you will be able to pull your senergy together in one place. Even though everyone has to take their own steps to succeed because some can use a thought in one way and someone else in another. As long as they are able to center the entire concept to grow from to develop the flower of the loveoutame.

M-N

The unusual thing is how great a squirrel's bite is compared to ours. A squirrel has 7 thousand psi's in a bite and a human has only several hundreds. The weird part is they are fury little cute things and we are huge creatures but we still don't know what to say sometimes. Maybe we need to expand our knowledge and we will have an ability to say the right things. What can this mean? Maybe nothing.

Was that something to give us a presence of taking a bigger bite out of things we are supposed to in different ways?

Smart News

Some news you will see in the future that would have been muse news (M-N) will now be called smart-news (S-N).

Therefore, do not accept any of Satan's laughoutame weeds. They may look like good but they are poison.

To let it be known: the loveoutame flower comes out of people on or as a spiritual presence through the heart. It is and can be seen and noticed at times and sometimes not so much. I don't know why some people have to have it develop in them and others don't but the good part is, it is everyone.

Death is a vital part of the social life but over kill is unhealthy in an ungodly way of doing it. Therefore, don't play with an action that God didn't give you permission to do. It might be the things that kill you in the end of your life.

One thing people do sometimes after killing someone is try to honor their posthumously that is unhelpful.

This is the best way I know how to put another nail in Satan's coffin. I hope you enjoy putting one or more in also by using the wisdom of the Lord in your life.

We have the job of stopping an increase that is an inside storm. It can be referred to as the inner-Cain in people. The more who get affected by it from a major incident the bigger the storm. An example of this was the loss of something or someone, like the young man who got killed by a police officer in Philadelphia. This brought the inner-Cain which comes from pain in people and nothing but satisfaction could calm it down. The police officer was indicted. Things calmed down but what is crazy is the police got caught in Satan's dieconomie.

If there is no satisfaction put in place after the fact Trump lost it will or could be like an inner-Cain that takes place. So to put up before a triage ahead of time would be the wise thing

America is an up-rooter of people, hundreds or thousands who are caught in a massive way of a thought that can guide them to become violent.

We can't present a herd of animals when they are on a stampede. With a calculated plan in hand it can make a difference with humans.

The other parts of learning to stop the inner-Cain as was when Cain killed Abel and to understand to stop the inner-Cain it makes us able to do more in the body of Christ along with stopping the dieconomie in a large number of people or do we present it as a way to stop people from raising Cain.

That is why if it has Cain in it, it can be deceitful sometimes, such as Cocaine, hurricane, inner-Cain that can be stopped with the loveinme power that also reflects the loveoutame flower. That is a cure and this is not a play on words. This lost gets to people one by one but if it gets to a group you have known what it could be like so we stop both levels of confusion to gain the control with understanding and love.

If someone learns to do this beforehand then it wouldn't happen as often. It is also the way to help stop childhood bullying to forgive in a divine order of love that helps to stop Satan's dieconomie. If Cain forgave either way he wouldn't have killed Abel. The fruit of the tree would become null and void. Forgive one's self for thinking wrong to stop the seed and action.

Satan can catch some people off guard and cause them to become bullet bullies and harm someone they didn't want to. Protect yourself let the loveoutame become a part of your life.

One way out

The old way of action is on a level of how the West was won and anyone can be a bullet bully in life with a gun and that is the Tommy gun way of thinking on the gangster way of negativity. That can change.

It is now so old and outdated only a fool lives by it's principles. So get out of a state of mind that reflects bad history and news and if you want to live learn to kill someone with love even if it calls for you to leave them at the altar.

M-N

We have the stop raising the hell-of-Cain up in life. Let it stay buried.

Change the tune

The worse kind of dieconomie to be caught up in is a dieconomie that hates a child. It may be for one or more, like you can't see the beauty in them you may not have the love to offer them. You may not want to put the time in then that is needed for whatever reason a better or big reason. You may not want to put the money in them that they would cost.

The reason could be endless but if you did you could have one of the best of the best friends in life that could ever be. If you feel like that gives up the child or use your imagination and see yourself opening up the door of a room that said exists to end the dieconomie door. Then go out and every time you feel like doing the wrong thing open the door in your mind and walk out and close the door no matter how many times it takes.

This door can be walked out of by anyone who has an ungodly need to want to kill someone or if you have the next biggest the dollar that can be a road way to cause evil. Get off the road and take the next exit sign. Use your imagination to build an off ramp in life that takes you away from the issues that want to try to harm you by way of you doing it to others.

There is one subject I didn't want to go to, but if we know the rules of not having intimacy or at least use protection the abortions could stop more daily. I don't exactly know if someone aborts a fetus whether it is subject to be a part of Satan's dieconomie.

Smart-News (S-N)

What causes the increase in violence? The copycat cop out sin-drome. It is what some people may be left with because of feeling alone and empty on the inside. That is why this wisdom make the cup run over to stop the intruder from coming in.

S-N

Another non-play on words. Why is it that some people think like they got good sense but don't feel like they got good sense? I think what they think may be only half true because if your feelings don't match your thinking it may be time for some new thinking.

S-N

The television show that came on, on Monday night July 8, 2018 was an episode that depicted an illusion of an election that was lost then the people began an uprising and the government had to put Marshall Law in effect. It is hoped not be a memory of what can take place in real life without the underlying detail about the true presence of the devil and his part his is waiting to play along with the facts of what we as Christian are to be doing before this can take place to stop and reject this kind of a dilemma of Satan.

It is the lack of knowledge that causes people to parish and this is the non-lethal way of doing things that can make peace. This can help get everyone on the same page without the testing, etc., using the Lord's way of telecommunication.

That is what the bullet bully party can do: it can create a revealing veil to take the pressure off of someone's life that has a kind of build-up of the death wish sindrome Satan can make a part of life because of the things that can keep damaging someone if they do I get a relief plan of action such as!!!

Have a bullet bully anti-violence party. Have a bury the bad bullet bully funeral it may be done without anyone's body. Just dig a hole as deep as you can and drop the bullets in it or find a safe place to leave the weapon and bullets.

There are different kinds of bullet bullies: school, gangs, robbers, police.

It automatically directs people to the Lord's turnpike that put people on track that goes in the right direction. It is time to have a bury a bullet funeral. It is a way to make it known you would rather waste the cost of a bullet than waste a priceless life. So dig a hole 1 foot by 1 foot by 4 to 6 feet and drop a bullet in it then thank God it is not a human going down.

Some may think I went a little overboard with the book #Enough and I say it is better to go over than not to if it will help with all in need.

Do you know there are some people who kill and really didn't want to? What happened is they fell under Satan's rule and got caught without the wisdom they need to stop themselves.

Catch this ball without a glove

You may have been beaten up and/or beaten down, shoved and kicked around but it doesn't matter because you are still loved. So don't let yourself get recruited in the wrong principles of thinking because it is better to be poor than rich in ways that cannot cost you a jail or hell sentence.

Don't let yourself get recruited into a bullying state of any kind of action. It can take your sight and make you blind and create dark days and empty nights that leave you on the outside of the world or life altogether.

Noting: the bola-bola and Anglo-bola dieconomie are a part of each other.

S-N

It is time to stop making yourself lame by maiming, crippling or killing others. You may be lame or cripple on the inside of your spirit. Get your fixer upper that the wisdom of the Lord has to help you get well so you can stop harming others.

The start of something good

We have to learn how to first face and defuse our anger. Then we have to learn how to face our having anxiety to want to control others when we are not in control as well as being pumped to not allow ourselves to understand how our emotions are getting out of hand. These three things can help us to create a better balance to be able to function on the norm.

How many people do you think may have PTSD (post-traumatic stress disorder) who have only developed this process of non-growth or an existing problem due to the governmental process of negativity that it is displaying out here that causes people to have an inner damaged nerve and also want to become warmongers because of this? This is a subliminal blind focus of possibility that may not exist. If it does exist maybe we can do a study on this we will have the answers because we have pre-arranged answers before the study.

What can we do to increase our chances to create happiness in dark dreary places where people do not want to set realistic goals for themselves or want to get motivated about being a part of life and the concept of contributing toward life because of the government's PTSD that it is putting on part of the population? We are trying to develop a plan to eliminate it and prevent it from taking over in certain segments of America which it seems to have done already.

This could be something that has affected rural and other communities throughout the country, not only the inner cities but in places where there may not be lots of development going on and where boredom may be happening. Boredom may be the workshop of Satan. We want to make sure it takes people out of an existence of a negative reality to a place where they can experience a new place of thinking clearly.

The bottom line is how much of the government's PTSD from their process of dysfunction does it cause others to have this illness that needs to be corrected? Whatever the numbers are we need to work on them and correct them so we do not lose a generation. I think this was also a problem for past generations that we may have lost because we did not have a correct sense of social and economic development that checks on it because we were blind to Satan sitting up in a high place as a towerist in government.

Some think some of the harm that is being done to people is because of the intensity of the decision making in our government.

I can never say that this is a complete cure all for everything that I have written about. I can say that I am testifying to the fact that I have had personal experience in lots of the areas I have written about. I have succeeded through spiritual wisdom and blessings to overcome the negativity that it helped wanted me to overcome.

The outside influence that I consider to be Satan I have a testimony to satisfy anyone in the area of trying to understand what the problem is. I still have certain thoughts that come into my head that I have to dismiss and realize that I am only human and negativity will jump into place if I let it and cause me to make a mistake of foolishness. When I put it all together I have basically graduated from the level of the numb-dumb void-noid sin-drome. Graduation yes but a complete cure and being totally whole, I cannot say, but I do not have any foolish acts from my thoughts. I am totally prepared to say "get thee behind me Satan."

Not good but true

The country was built off of people who were bullet bullies the culture of America was the same but life was made from people that the Lord made from his love. Love power can stop the presence of anyone being a bullet bully in life.

The fix is here

It is like if we don't take the time to help the bullies, which we might say is our enemy, and love and teach them why they are the way they are, then we are the bullies and we may not look like it but. They are trapped by the prince of darkness or lost in some kind of madness or fake reality. We are at fault if we don't help them. We need to start eliminating as many bullies as we can.

I think the next step up from the loveoutame process of growth is the agape. Therefore we are closer to where we should be now that we have received this wisdom.

I can admit when I am wrong even though it does not feel good. There may be the eros and philia processes of love. To put this in the right perspective, you will have to do the research to find out where the eros and philia falls and generates energy to bring about change along with the loveoutame and agape love.

This process of thinking regarding the opponent being their only enemy has led to the dimension of the presence of where only the Lord knew that there would be those who were their own enemy due to the influence of Satan. The Lord did not want them to be left out of the equation of their eternal well being but the process he had to develop was the upcoming revelation.

There are some who will be fighting die-hardedly until the end and they cannot win nor can they reach the inside gates of heaven. This has to become a part of where the future generations will have to wake up so they will not be a part of the mess if they want to be a part of the process of seeing God's face.

One of the biggest problems is fear. They are afraid to let go of what they are used to. They figure if they let it go good, bad or indifferent thinking, they will drop straight off the planet by losing their balance. This is foolishness. When you know you are not right try to let God come into your life. That will serve the purpose of eliminating fear, anxiety, frustration and all the things that go along with the way things were.

Who am I as a Christian if I know a pathway that others need to get on in order to walk themselves out of darkness but will not share it with them? I am only one who looks over the part of mankind that does not have the true real love that is supposed to be shared in Jesus' name. If you are one who knows the pathway but you are not sharing it with others, then you are slacking and lacking. That is not healthy for humanity or the Body of Christ.

One of the problems that people have is when they understand there is negativity in someone and don't know how to get it out. They want to kick the abomination out of them. They become hostile and even though they want to feel positive, they are portraying negativity that wants to come back. You can't kick abomination out of someone. You have to expose them to the love of God using God's wisdom. It is the truth that will set them free not kicking the Cain out of them. Even though I must admit it sounds good, it is still bullshit to try to kick the Cain out of someone.

I have personally felt like kicking the Cain out of someone because I could be kicking it out of myself. I do not think the same way as I did when I thought I was too grown to be a child of God but not anymore because it almost sent me to hell.

There is one thing I can say that does not make me feel good. I have known people who were afraid to go through necessary things in order to be who they were meant to be. Some even committed suicide or hurt so much which was a part of Satan's dieconomie.

We have to wipe out the fear factor of being present in the future as well as not being afraid of the upcoming hellacost that some will have to pay in order to make it through the revolution. We should accept it as God's way of returning to clear the air and settle the debt to show Satan that he is owed nothing. We have to keep as many of us safe as we can. That is the major job to keep us safe and out of Satan's grip of torment and torture so he cannot have our eternal souls.

Once this level of wisdom is revealed to you and you accept it, you have what could be known as a key to conquer Satan and to keep him away from causing you destruction. The key comes from being blessed just as all humans should be.

The question is: are you one of those who don't know what you have done or are doing to yourself? If so, then you are unable to forgive yourself. But now that you may understand what you may be doing or have done to yourself you can forgive yourself. That is a great part of achieving your goals in life. You can't move on to the future until you can close the door on your past and leave it behind.

The one thing I can honestly say is, no matter how you feel about the country, it should not let you down or cause you to live up to or above your own expectations. No one was made as a disaster area or a person of no capability of creating reasoning powers. The fact of you being one who may have been living in poverty, which is where Satan wants you to be, is something you need to be aware of.

Be proud you live in the USA, it has done more for the human race than can ever be told. Help it to not become a fraud from within itself so others will discontinue association with them.

It is okay to think of having first your patriotic presence of understanding and homage to your spirit of all in life. I mean first after the Lord. The Lord is always first.

It is time to create super duper success
in stopping Satan's dieconomie

Twenty-four seven

Every time you feel like picking up a pistol or want to do something wrong, use this therapy: imagine there is a blackboard in front of you. On the blackboard the word bullet bully is there. Erase it every time you think about taking a gun out or doing someone harm. Look at the blackboard and use the eraser to get rid of it. Keep this in your mind and it will help. It is guaranteed you will succeed.

There is someone I almost killed at high school that I still see from time to time. I am glad I didn't harm them. That person was a bad person back then and now they are not.

It is clear that the killing some youth, and others, by police for no legitimate reason is a part of Satan's dieconomie that was precipitated by the shooters. It can't be legitimized in any other way other than this: whether they get away with it or not on the earthly level it will not fly in heaven.

I believe some people were caught off guard and really didn't mean to harm others. Satan likes to destroy as many lives as he can.

The children can be taught to stop being bullies if we can get adults do things we don't talk about, such as passing along or sharing this kind of information, then we can make positive change.

There are many adults being some kind of bully on many levels: sexual, mental, physical or verbal abuse. The book *Time to Stop the Abuse* can help them. Some people need this kind of help to stop bullying. Abusive people are bullies too. So let's put a stop to all bullying and help break the cycle.

This should be known and understood: once you have accepted the fact of being a part of the loveoutame generation you can understand that the loveoutame friend is a kind of cupid. It is somewhat mythical but real. It allows itself to project love toward others even the ones they don't like. It is just a natural fact. One of cupid's best friends is Zeus. Once you discover who that is you become an ancient miner of spiritual myths. This leads you in a pathway of touching reality.

You have the opportunity to become a sky chief disciple or a hooded saint disciple. That can lead you on the pathway of becoming a sapphire blue blooded priest of the ecumenical order. It will grant you the blessings to be able to show others the way to succeed and gather on a peaceful level.

.

The loveoutame is the most powerful positive avenue of creating the conduit within one's self of God's love being shared and showered around, among and upon people.

You can get some of the greatest stimulation of edification to your soul and spirituality from this process of the loveoutame dimension of trust, truth and reality. Its good friend cupid who aligns itself with Zeus in turn aligns itself as a spiritual miner. It digs into spirituality to give positivity back to the earthly realm. You can stretch out into that atmosphere to receive and share as a sky chief disciple, hooded saint disciple and/or a sapphire blue blooded priest.

It is now time to cause the fall of complex realities that want to keep us confused. We must level the playing field so that we don't lose balance of our true perspective of our eternal well-being. We must keep kingdom building and the bride of Christ, which is the church, in tact.

The loveoutame state of growth can become a ritual to be practiced on a daily basis by simply saying "I intend to deliver as much of the loveoutame as I can to my fellow man at any place and any time."

We are to encourage each other to learn more about earth's epic journey through space and through the dimension of growth. We should learn about love that is being projected daily and eliminate as much negative activity as we can. We can accomplish this thanks to the loveoutame which will hopefully put that love into you.

This process that has been developed through forces of nature gives us a better understanding of us riding our own spaceship which happens to be earth. It is a part of the force of nature that we are involved in throughout the universe. Let's just enjoy the ride without causing destruction and try to love our planet more and more daily.

Who needs another kind of space ship when we are living in the best possible space ship and adventure that there ever could be in existence. Anything on top of this may have a challenge to it but it is not as exciting. It will never give you the emotional ride that exhilerates you to want to become a part of the daily activities in life in the world we live in.

Empathy, which is a part of the loveoutame process, needs to be expressed. Empathy may come between cupid and the loveoutame or it may come between Zeus and the loveoutame. The creative skills, that are spiritual skills that may lie between the loveoutame, have the greatest assets toward fellow man. They will help make the plan greator and better in life in order for success to be experienced.

I hope this wisdom will be forever on time, in the name of the Lord.

I may be one of the most unorthodoxed writers of all time. I never had the professionals go in front or behind me. Being at somewhat of a crossroad I may have missed something I would have liked to do for you. So forgive me if you feel there is something missing, there is one thing in there for sure, the love of God.

This is a healthy adult way to keep growing up and maturing with an understanding of how to share love and stop the hating on others.

One of the latest victims of the process of getting caught up in Satan's dieconomie is the man who lost his life to the mother of his kids. The real victims are the two children. Family violence that leads to the killing of a space is also abuse to the extreme. But it is the goal of the devil. His plan is the trap people in his dieconomie. he book I wrote titled _Time to Stop the Abuse_, whether mental, physical, verbal or sexual gives the guidance to help prevent family violence from happening and stop abuse on all levels.

Effects of Towerism

The effects of those who are affected by someone's towerism has no boundaries. It can take over someone to crossover to anyone that is human, and go up in their place of worship to cause harm, as was done to the 11 people in a particular incident of violence.

I feel in my heart the need to help heal their hearts.

Do not think a man of another kind of faith can not bring relief to you, especially if he was sent by the Lord as a messenger.

This is a part of *The Biggest Collar*

With all of the information that was put together, It will make you able to help stop Satan in his tracks as well as to help stop a part of his dieconomie. Now we all can collar him, but the people who may be following him, that do not know he is setting up a trap for them, need the information in this book to help stop Satan from bullying people into becoming bullies, which is what he does if he gets to the unprotected.

Now can we look at this message as a great opportunity for us to get a little smarter in ways to help us come together. If you ever heard the statement, "I will bless the Lord," here is your chance.

Our goal in life may be to become an anti-bullet bully advocate to help stop the invisible footprint of Satan's dieconomie from becoming a part of the reality of someone's life. This can be done if you are open to a level of being desensitized to the life matters presence of living.

It is unbelievable to think that bullying exists, but it does. There are some people who think that life does not matter. It is because they need a better understanding of life and how much it matters. It comes from the wisdom to be used that the Lord supplies.

To keep it real, too many people make it too much of a challenge to learn about God's wisdom, even some from within the house of God. Some people shy away from the teaching. They are the ones in most cases who are desensitized to the love process of growing up in life. They keep a childish attitude and think that because of their age the things that they are doing it is okay. That is the furthest from the truth. It leaves them open to the void-noid, numb-dumb, sin-drome in life. This is how Satan comes in to introduce them to his way to thinking, doing, and living, and if the opportunity comes they are recruited to do the bad thing, being a devil. They get blindsided and are at a loss, causing some other people pain, because of their acting out as a child in a devilish way. That's just what Satan wants. He looks forward to decreasing the angels in heaven. This is his way of doing it, he may get one or two, it doesn't matter, when we can do our best to not let him get any.

I have spent over half of my lifetime putting together a plan through the wisdom supplied by the Lord that can help people get free from that bondage of Satan. The tools are in the books I write, and they can be used by anyone. It is time to know what you may not know about being a real adult in life. To start, try _A Message From the Word._ It is a church in the book I've written.

Take note, Know that words matter, in this a crisis? Yes. If it is one life that can be saved from this disease of a spiritual kind to help put a part of life back on track, because it has gotten off track in matters of life and death. The right words have potential to create an anti-inflammatory that gives a common affect such as if someone was on the drug Tubocorarine, a relaxant. It also can develop the ingrates of a response like immunoslimulatory as if using a root like the danggui, also the dong quai, of Chinese medicine.

Some people can think of this as kind of science because of its direct topics! Our life science for the non-scientist. How nice to be able to look at both sides of the coin.

The key to things may be if we want to become stronger than hate, we have to become smarter than hate, and that's where we are now. Becoming smarter than hate, so we can become stronger than hate. That is what the world needs now, to be strong in love.

It is a part of love to become stronger than hate. It is a part of loveoutame to become stronger than hate. It is a part of understanding how to stop the dieconomie to become stronger than hate. It is a part of understanding the footprint of Satan so that he will not keep walking over this planet, walking over through and out of nations leaving pain of all kinds, by becoming stronger than hate, but we have to become smarter than hate first. The power of loveoutame does that. That is what people are showing, but they need to understand it even greater with this wisdom that is being placed in this material in these books.

To understand man's spiritual nature may be one of the greatest gifts he can ever possess. To be able to develop the concept of how the spiritual DNA takes place, and works, and find the nucleus, is a part of that understanding. I will consider it having three parts the loveoutame first, the hateoutame next or the natureoutame, to be able to put that in a nucleus of understanding, which continually spins around within the spiritual realm of a person. This occurs without them knowing it is a way to develop the strength that we have that we can use. If we don't understand it, it can defeat us because if the nucleus of the atom itself is disturbed by a thing like trauma or a downfall of some kind, it affects actions being good or not good. That is why we keep the loveoutame on top.

When the spiritual atom slows down to a pace where it is sitting on one level, such as if a person has spiritual skills it keeps the feeling of never hating. It defeats you personally, and as it spins around you never want it to slow down where it gets on that level sitting up on hate. We always want to manage it so that it is sitting up on the level of lovoutame on top of the loveoutayou, so the hate wont come out of you.

People get confused with the loveoutame with the sex nature out of them, so know sex out of you is not loveoutayou. That's one thing that has to be cleared up and kept in perspective at all times as a pyramid.

Am I some kind of theorist? Have I stumbled on something through constant study and prayer hoping I can help make this place a better place, or the people better people. I want to help people discover the DNA that's on the outside of us and the spiritual realm of things that are on the inside. They combine and unite, and always growing more closer together, one way or another. Time cannot tell, what can tell is the reality of the faith that you have and how it can help you to survive the sin-dromes that are in the world, as we identify with the hand we are dealt and use the genetic markers we are born with.

Can we look at this as some type of emergency? I think so, or need, or desire, or something we have to have growth in, it is like for instance we could have as humans a blood drive to get the necessary ingredients for to maintain life.

Now we need a spiritual drive of the understanding to get the word out about the DNA. We need to get the word out about the nucleus and the genetic part of this while using old spiritual development.

Saving lives, saving spirits, saving someone from having to go to hell, all adds up to the same thing: the loveoutaus and the love out of you that God gives us.

Can the loveoutame process help to end the desires that are negative in life, such as drug use, suicide, abuse, or anything that's on the other side of the positive level of wealth? I do believe so. It's like having a degree of a miracle that is growing in you to preserve the reality of self preservation, and also share it with others.

Could this be considered the dieconomie code? No, it is the loveoutame code that breaks the dieconomie into pieces. It deletes its existence in a reality of a multitude of people. It makes them aware of the presence of what a satanic presence can not do when you know what it's trying to do, what it wants to do, and what it is setting you up to accomplish. The new code of the loveoutame to break the dieconomie code is what it's all about.

For some

The criteria for this greater presence of reality requires only to keep things simple. The process that we are obtaining now is uncomplicating the development of harassment in a presence of unknown seen reality. That reality has been in the atmosphere due to the negativity that has a force field that people can't see or get through unless they have spiritual skills. Those skills are developed through God's wisdom.

Now that we have a new presence of a way out of a way of being trapped in a place that has no locks, no gates, no keys. It only has a presence of a development of an atmosphere that may seem somewhat stigmatized. That is what takes place. We become stigmatized on an atmosphere that's unseen in our presence and we get locked into it. Now we are free from this bondage, in Jesus name, Amen.

Some would say how sweet it is to be loved by someone, and that someone is you. So realize how sweet it is to be loved by you. This is the icing on the cake that has been baked in heaven and presented to mankind. You can't see it, but you can feel it. If you try hard enough you can taste the sweetness of this kind of success, that cannot affect your life in the wrong way, again Amen and Hallelujah.

Some would say it cut the preaching and teaching to the chase, and I would say it is just only a measure of love. It is a part of the iceberg that sits on the bottom. Still individuals need to go to the house of God to share fellowship so they can get a topside point of view on the directions they should be going in. I am a part of the preacher and teacher but this is the bottom side of the iceberg. Get topside so you can hit the top and the bottom, so you have to be stuck in between in the middle, and get all squashed in.

It's a great time to realize you have locked down the elements that Satan tries to use against you.

Now you can blow him literally out the water. He has no ground to stand on, float on or appear on. He disappears, because he has vanished into oblivion and out of your zone. You are no longer in one of Satan's zones.

There are two frames of thought. One is the presence of Satan came to place his footprint on mankind to kill steal and destroy in the garden of Eden. The way he did the most harm went to another level. It was after the Lord took down the Tower of Babel. That is when people were disappointed in the Lord because he stopped them. Satan stepped in to take advantage of that. It may sound simple but it was the catalyst that created towerism.

If you happen to think that this may some kind of adventure, you could be right. It does have the makings of understanding the footprints as they are walking toward a pathway in a way that unveils certain elements to be recognized as facts to learn from and grow out from a misunderstanding that you may have about this material or to be able to put your own perspective on it which is okay. So an adventure with excitement that gives you a thrill as you gravitate toward a new horizon to be able to become wiser at your own pace and have the advantage of acknowledging things as you see fit. This is what it is all about.

This is an independent study that you can present to yourself to become more aware of the things that are happening in the world, in life and in spiritual development. Enjoy it don't just read it with a set presence that you can't get something from it or you will perceive it as something that is not real. Try to find what is real to you because it is the best thing for you when you do it on your own and with the right context you can do anything as long as it is broken down into terminology that puts it on a laymen level.

As for me, I may be just a kind of way to take to another as you learn to see your way out to a place that has made a way out of no way. If we learn from the Lord to stop Satan from bullying people, people won't do it to others.

Is this a part of some kind of development of a hypothesis? I don't think so. The loveoutame is to be considered protons. The negativity is considered to be neutrons.

We have learned to become the latest and updated patriots in a new frame of America because time is up for the old way of existing. Not meaning to sound tilted but can we produce the McGyverism to stop the dieconomie in its tracks? I can think we can, no, I know we can.

We have to understand that we are now in the stage of delivery from an unseen plantation. This plantation is a place where a state of reality has been tainted and torn and infiltrated by the worse bully of them all. His name happens to be Satan. He bullies people on all levels. He has bullied people who are suppose to have responsibility and authority and is no respecter of persons as the Lord is. The Lord did not give any man that kind of authority. That is why we have to take our sights and look to another means of stopping the bullying, madness and sadness.

If we truly are our brothers' keepers then we look at them as a spiritual creation first and not what they have become in mankind's existence, whether they are butcher, baker, preacher, teacher, police, mayor or president.

We know that in some ways we all have been damaged and when we look at anyone, we need to first look at them as how damaged they are and you can't find that out until you know who the person is. In order for you to be able to clear the pathway you must look at yourself as your brothers' keepers then you look at the damage inside of you and what has damaged you. Then maybe there is a glimmer of hope that you can bring about a better understanding.

101

We have to realize that if we are at war with ourselves in one way or another, we have to learn to not project that on others. The spiritual warfare that goes on causes more of Satan's footprint and we have to eliminate as much of it as we possibly can. What I am saying is when you look at someone, look at them as a spiritual being who may be damaged more than you no matter who they are or what their authority may be. Then if you perceive them in that way it delivers you from being one who is pointing your fingers. You don't have to predetermine that they are your enemy and can never be your friend.

This will help you see how we misplace each other

Therefore, the controversy in the judgment and the laws that has been set forth before you and them are already in place. There is no opportunity for you to be able to come to a conclusion or agreement that you can be civil to each other. We can understand that if there is a situation we have to solve it in a meaningful existence and not let it escalate beyond recognition of having someone lose control and become demonized in a presence. What we do from there is stop the whole process as we approach ourselves consistently.

We are on this plantation of satanic behavior because that is what it is if you are not looking on a positive level or if you don't have any spiritual development which is skills, you have to look at it as yourself first and develop the loveoutayou first. So when you approach someone you can see the love in them no matter who they are or what they have done or how you feel because that is the way it is supposed to be.

Now we are getting off this plantation because the miracle has taken place and the miracle to spread this justice of the injustice starts with the miracle in you. There are some procedures and developmental processes that have to be gone through. We have to become educated and we need to become knowledgeable and aware of ourselves and then we can become aware of others.

If we are going through something, as I have been through, I would say dozens of traumatic experiences in my life before I could even present this I had to develop a way to present the loveoutame and the Lord has blessed me with that, even though I had to pay a hell of a cost.

I could help a multitude of people who are going through it if they understand and obey the rules and regulations that are governed by the Lord and mankind's laws you can always have in place without having to deal with them in an obnoxious way of making them your enemy and breaking them.

This is one of Satan's plans. He wants you to break mankind's laws so mankind can have a reason to intrude on your space and eliminate you from your space that is not supposed to be (or have you) incarcerated.

We can develop the steps to move forward and take down these walls that have been put up between us and the walls that tell us that we are locked on a plantation. We are now going to be planting the loveoutame seeds throughout our hearts and hopefully they will go or grow throughout the world one day.

The matador's cape has just been retired. For anyone who refuses to retire it, they may be retarded. What do I mean by the matador's cape? It is like the people who come out of their homes and the officers who come out to do their job have a confrontation and someone has the cape up already. The cape basically has the red sign of blood with a sword of some kind behind it to harm someone. This is them basically putting up a red flag saying, "I'm looking for a fight. I'm looking forward to seeing if I can defeat or kill the bull in you."

Let's look at things in another perspective. If someone has trauma, or they have been through something, they are automatically lifted up where their feet are not planted on the ground. What takes place then is the balloon fills with helium and raises them up. This is because of a trauma. The more trauma that they are unable to resist they get another balloon lifting them up higher. This is anyone at any time that could be facing this. At the same time, they are trying to figure the problem out and come back down to earth but they are unable to.

Negativity is all about taking someone off balance, putting the fear in them, not giving them an opportunity to get their balance. They are afraid of their own self-destruction or someone else destroying them. They become apprehensive and repulsive and defensive to others. What do we do to help end this? We have to realize that there may be a curse from their forefathers. They may have an insecurity or a misguided compass in life where they don't really understand what they are doing or where they need to be.

We hope to give people insight but first look at them as someone who was or could have been lost before they understood how to become a spiritual being, someone who has a presence of being able to find a way to resolve issues. We have to look at them as our brothers' and we are their keepers.

Instead of coming out with a cape when we walk out of the house we come out with a cupid bow and arrow. As we see someone or are confronted with someone who we feel will cause negativity to take place we automatically are shooting out our arrows into the balloons and release the helium so they can come back down to earth so they can be planted firmly on ground. They will know that both them and you are harmless.

This is how God's therapy works

What has developed is the loveoutame cupid syndrome that has taken place to head off, stop and defeat the negative process of coming into a situation. If we all think about the loveoutame cupid syndrome before re we leave home each morning or even at home between family members, we may find ourselves living in a better world than we ever thought we could live in, rather than living with a red indication as if we want war or we want to fight the bull or we intend to get the bull out of you.

We have been approaching things in the wrong way for centuries. This has become a part of Satan's plan for us to continue living this way. This is why we are losing so many people in the dieconomie process.

Venture not out of your space until you have understood that you have cupid's bow and arrows to deflate the helium. Once you have understood these facts, look up and see how many balloons filled with helium have been lifted above your head and taken your feet off the ground and you can start shooting them down.

To use the kind of metaphor to help end a level of spiritual war is good therapy and all it takes is a vivid imagination.

The bottom line with the work I do is, the Lord equipped me after I became a willing vessel. You are really the ones who had me hired to do this because it was something that needed to be done. We needed someone who could put it in a format that all could understand.

I am a crisis intervention specialist but you are really the one who has to denounce the principles that Satan has put upon your life. I am thankful to you if you work with me or hire me. I am also thankful to the Lord for allowing me to be the vessel he uses to guide you through an era of ungodliness and negativity to reassess and redevelop a cultural status to overcome anything that comes to us by way of one of Satan's storms.

I am thankful for the opportunity and then you show me the loveoutayou. I can't ask for anything more than maybe a pittance to help me survive through the trying times.

I hope it is something that you feel good about: the fact that this is really your idea in the first place. Throughout generations we have developed prayers. Your idea is to get answers to prayers and these are the answers that you have been given by the blessings of the Lord. You have prayed for someone to bring an answer as they prayed for Jesus, the Messiah, the King to relieve pressure, torment, trouble and hellish situations on earth.

The Lord has made mini me's. A mini me is basically someone who has been given the Lord's foresight because of prayers, to be able to give relief to the body of Christ and increase justice for all in many different ways. As I would say, I am just a branch off of the tree. There are other branches coming off of me and I thank God for them.

Could we say this is your loveoutame that is taking place because of your prayers and the writing that I do? I think we can. I also think we can be safe in our sound decision-making.

There is nothing like a sound state of mind and a heart filled with joy and a spirit that soars like you are still a little boy or girl. There is nothing in the world to compare to those feelings when you share them with others and you have a true idea of who you are.

Now that you have become educated you can become an educator. No longer are you polarized or stigmatized or drowning in the victim's level of not knowing. You are able to speak boldly with the principles that guide you to a stronger person that you have always been.

As we say, we lose a little something out here because Satan is like cryptonite. We are super people in our own ways. We have come through the evolution of becoming more humane daily. We never want to lose that. We want to keep moving forward. In other words, the spiritual skills kill cryptonite as on placement in a sense of sins and Satan.

Now we develop our own new and better concepts as we move forward into a new millennium, especially being the individuals who are receiving the change of the world's perspective and has a responsibility of putting it back into a place where it needs to be. Become not just learned, become a teacher and a sponsor to yourself so you can show someone else how to do what you do as the Lord would do.

Is the part of mankind lost as God's infants who never make it to be a child of God? Could they be called a SIDS child since they may have died before they were safe with the blessing of the safety of the Lord?

They say there's no rest for the weary. So be at rest today and get enough always.

Luke 11:2
2. So He said to them, "When you pray, say: Our Father in heaven, hallowed be Your name. Your kingdom come, Your will be done on earth as it is in heaven.

To get some grace and mercy just say Father I am here. Know that God is mercy, God's love.

Hebrews 4:15-16
15. For we do not have a High Priest who cannot sympathize with our weaknesses, but was in all points tempted as we are, yet without sin.
16. Let us therefore come boldly to the throne of grace, that we may obtain mercy and find grace to help in time of need.

The best thing about this work is it lets you know that God is love.

John 4:8, 11, 24
8. For His disciples had gone away into the city to buy food.
11. The woman said to Him, "Sir, the well is deep. Where then do You get that living water?"
24. "God is Spirit, and those who worship Him ust worship in spirit and truth."

Know that God is spirit. What is mercy? It is God's desire to better the tree of life in you, then you desire that. God can do it for you so you should do it for others.

A relationship with the father requires us to share the love God gives us all. The greatest thing you can do to keep the father with you is say to him, "hello, I am here to be in your will."

If you are forgiven for your sins then you should also forgive others, even before they commit a sin. It may stop a sin that someone may want to commit against someone else. The actions that come out of your heart is all the Lord looks at.

I have come to some conclusions about the justice system. Let's look at it as a secondary frame of existence and look at God's laws first as the real justice system. If anyone does not understand them or participate in them in the proper manner, they fall into the next element of the system which is the justice system that man created.

Maybe God's laws were created for individuals to follow so they wouldn't fall under mankind's laws. If it is injustice that someone must receive before they receive justice, they need to therefore learn the justice of God's laws so they won't fall into mankind's laws and be under his jurisdiction.

It may sound strange in a way but it may just be a warning or an element of development that some people will have to go through mankind's laws and understand how to stop breaking those laws before they can understand how they work and sit down long enough and relate them to God's laws. In other words, it is like one hand washes the other in a context of you don't understand yet that if you get God's laws straight you won't have to deal with man's laws.

It is sort of a catch 22 because I think about the furniture industry and how they used formaldehyde, a poison, to build furniture. At the same time, the whole thing coincided to me I realize that this could be one of the problems that caused lots of SIDS of death in babies from them having the life choked out of them from the formaldehyde because of them not being adapted to that atmosphere. I am going to do some research and I would appreciate it if someone else could do some research also.

How many babies may have been affected and may have expired prematurely? When you turn it back to mankind's problems, how many of mankind were prematurely put into a justice system to find their way to a system of spiritual growth in order for them to not miss the Godly presence that has developed in their lives when they have been locked up? It makes you want to think and I am thankful to be able to think and help others think.

We have to get detoxified from the toxins that are here in order to continue to grow in the ways we need to. The detoxification can come from being incarcerated but we never needed to be detoxified of sin by meeting death because there is no justice after it is over with for some. We have to maintain the stay-ability so we can get the credibility as we need to protect the child from sudden crib death and SIDS if we can.

M-N

Lord can I find a way for you to bind me up with your boundless love. If I can find a way it would be the best day of my life.

Never fear the two-fold blindness that may take place in your life. Sometimes we can't see into darkness but darkness can see into us. So that is why we have to have an ever increasing light of God shining so that darkness can't see into us and work its way out of us. In order for us to prevent it from working its way out of us we need to be able to have a light on the inside which is the Lord. Do take this for granted because this is the truth and the truth is everlasting and is the light.

To look at things from another perspective, I must realize that Satan has developed a system where he puts people in a position to be in the dark thinking they are doing good by creating violence and harm toward others as if they are de-weeding the earth's garden of one of mankind's problems. What they are doing in retrospect is causing lives to be taken and on the other level jeopardizing individual's eternal well-beings. They have been put into a dimension of being so lost from the reality of the loveoutathem process because of the hatred and evil that is festering throughout the land in people that they are destroying some of God's loveoutause and it is not fair.

We have to wake up to the reality that you may be totally wrong while thinking you are right. So re-think your rights and wrongs.

What may be one of the biggest strategies that Satan uses when he recruits individuals to kill, steal and destroy? Whether it is harming or killing others it is the fact that he wants them to be totally blinded to what they have in their eyes. What they may be facing that they don't want to face that causes problems for them and others. He wants them to look directly at someone else and get the mote out of their eyes of whatever they did wrong. In other words, it makes people want to punish someone else and they may need punishment themselves.

The Lord forgives but Satan takes that part away, especially with individuals who think they are doing something great within themselves becoming a bullet bully or any other kind. It is foolish and ignorant but people are still stuck on stupid and believe they are doing something great.

It is time to end all of this talk and get things worked out and understood to fix this problem. We are no longer under the control of the demonology of Satan's principles that has put so many people in hell.

It is time to exhale all of the garbage, foolishness, wickedness and hatred and being maladjusted out of one's system and bring in the flower of the loveoutame that was supposed to be there in the first place. This earth was supposed to be free of all that until Satan's jealousy came down because he tried to take over heaven. He has taken over a part of the earth but now we are taking back that part of earth which has blinded so many individuals to the reality of death beating life and death never won over life. Jesus won over that death which allows us to be winners over it also.

There are still so many people who are at a loss of wisdom people are still going to hell. Now freedom is knocking at your door. It is kicking it in so please be aware that there is a new way of thinking, breathing, living, learning, teaching the old process is new. The earth has just been reorganized and recovered with a new freedom that we must learn in order to strive and survive even more than we ever have before.

I guess that is an end to Satan's plot thanks to the wisdom that the Lord supplies us with.

Muse–News

Don't hesitate to converse about this

M-N

The cake got baked in heaven it has also been sliced and put on the plate. Now all you have to do is eat it and savor the sweetness. Learn how to share it with others and serve it up wherever you go. The cake is made out of ingredients from a flower that is out of you the loveoutause flower that the flour that comes out of the grain.

This is a different cultural blend that has a sweetness unlike any other. To be able to put the love of the Lord into the presence of nurturing yourself with edification of wisdom and the pursuit of happiness is a wonderful experience.

The Bible divides Satan's principles so that we can conquer them. That is what I am emulating with the work I do; dividing Satan's principles so that we can conquer them.

In another format and another style but basically the same ideology.

Because he does have principles in order to elevate or de-elevate his kingdom building process by taking the people who are supposed to be going to heaven, causing them to put themselves in hell. What we are doing is unfolding his plan of devastation and destruction and making a new plan to stay away from it with this wisdom we have received from the Lord.

In other words, we are taking down a part of Satan's kingdom now. We are unequipping him by rebuilding what he has used for so many centuries to destroy mankind. We should be rejoicing and delighted to celebrate this new era.

This is like taking a one-way street that Satan has put the one way sign on and turned it around. It is saying now it is a two-way to allow you to come back out of it or turn around to come out of it. Get smart and don't go down it in the first place. There are warning signs all over it through the wisdom that is being placed here. Do not enter it is not necessary. Payback is not your job.

Do not choose the deathoutame flower that Satan plants and wants you to grab hold of instead of the loveoutame one.

Is this a part of the big picture that Satan's dieconomie flower has to be taken out of the picture and in order for us to spread the new way of growth throughout the country and the world. This will help us be able to stop personal wars and wars of multitudes of people in order for us to do one thing, be prepared for the upcoming rapture.

We will have enough people to constantly lose their eternal well-being through this process that will be taking place possibly sometime in the next 100 years. If we start working on it beforehand and expose Satan's plan to unbalance it so we can get as many people ahead of it as we can before he takes them into his existence, we have an opportunity to gather more of the flock in kingdom building to be bound to heaven.

Now what we have is a big picture of what needs to be done. We start off one by one with telling this news, this revelation, this new appreciation for life and justice for everyone, not the justice that was built by man but the justice for the system that has been put in place by the Lord. We can keep moving forward to greater things as the body of Christ and humanity itself.

This also can be considered a reality check on something that is better than the gold rush better than mining the diamond mines. This is the priceless stuff that the world was really made of. All of these other things on a material level is just compensation to a certain measure. Now we have discovered how to eliminate some of Satan's footprints and stop him from marching victoriously into the future in a way that he wanted to and know that everyone is counted in.

We have the real routes and pathways for us to be able to travel down in a harmonious, peaceful and loving manner instead of walking into the one-way dieconomie and accepting a flower of death.

Now we can present each other with a bonafide substance of a mannerism that can bring about a pleasant pursuit toward happiness. This is a journey that we have and all need to be migrating toward to not curse the future. This was done before to not put the wrong revelations in place to not be left behind in understanding can be one of the greatest things that we can possess now because we are on a pathway to heaven.

To prepare those who will meet the rapture to be able to stand up with the right principles by using the loveoutame flower in themselves to make this right for them and others. It can't be about self it has to be about us. This is what being a grown child of the Lord is all about.

Need not say more. Actions speak louder than words. Show me beats tell me so let's get it done.

This is a new chapter in mankind's ability to outgrow the negative possibilities. The new chapter is here to be told.

How to win this war is be prepared for it in a way that Satan never expected. That is what this is all about to be prepared for war that Satan doesn't know about and therefore can't win.

There has now been a new cake created, the disciple maker flower the sky is the limit flower the sky chief disciple flower, the hooded saint flower, the sapphire blue blooded priest or cleric flower, and there are more to complete the bouquet.

You could say you have just taken or opened the doors of one of God's kitchen. He has all of the ingredients that he blends love with in order to bring forth a new day for a victory for his children.

A new development of nourishment to keep us safe, happy and full of joy. This is the truth he wants you to know.

The prayers have been answered the orders have been given to us to forgive and receive God's divine wisdom. This is a part of God's intervention that has now placed a marshal law of the angels to help create miracles so people can know the Lord more because he is full of mercy. If there be one who has on a pair of Satan's blinders, take them off to witness to others.

If someone is in a spiritual war with themselves it has to be repaired. This came from no spiritual wisdom being applied to their life. We give them a kind of jump start to help by showing them a way to the intercessor b.k.a. Holy Spirit and it will put the light in place to move them out of darkness. It is like the home run that won the game in the Lord's name. I give this an explanation of therapy.

When it gets down to re-tooling, people are in different ways too cynical about changing because the fear of not knowing themselves or having to get to know someone who they did not want to have a relationship with in the first place. The faith building process comes in to take away the enemy that is fear that puts people in a self-incarcerated jail inside their head that is a war they have to fight. It spills out into life. So people have problems with others and that should not be a part of life. This is why the Lord puts spiritual skills together to give out keys to people to unlock themselves to know freedom.

The keys are information to present the truth of God's wisdom. This is presented in the mind your mind sight ministry of self that leads people to learn new things to help them grow stronger in order to withstand the devil that wants to destroy and harm people.

It is time to reveal the spiritual healthcare that is available in the United States.

The preacher gives a word present that enhances the words of a part of what is going on in the mind your mind sight ministry.

People still need to know this is a two-way street to keep the peace. If no one lives by the sword, the death count would drop dramatically behind the red cape there is no longer a sword.

Satan has three strikes or more. One is as you drop the cape and step on it because now the thought of having a weapon behind it is null and void. Also, as you stop looking at the mote in someone else's eye and clear your own eye you have given him a second strike.

The third strike is when you use cupid's arrow to release the helium out of the balloon so the individual can get their feet planted on solid ground. You also build their confidence to stay on a positive level at the same time you are building yours. Three strikes and he is out. He has lost the ball game and we don't have to play with him anymore.

Is this one of God's greatest
inventions to produce intervention?

At BTHPM, we do not want to know anyone's name who chooses to give an essay on the books.

Well, it is a problem that has existed since mankind began and we have to get better at developing ways to handle it. This work I do is hopefully another feather in the hat of the history of humanity. We must believe in one another of we don't have a chance to move forward.

As I said in one of my books, all it takes sometimes is all you have to do is identify with someone's problem and it lets them know they are not alone. It began to repair itself within and it may not have been fully known by them at the time that they were dealing with it. It is like the God's spirit in people can heal its people.

M-N

People must maintain the ability to not sell their soul for one ounce of gold.

M-N

Another process of action meets me at the center of the bridge that takes place in your heart.

M.Y.M.S.

We are the now people. We live with the principles of never making a molehill into a mountain and are equipped to with spiritual skills to make a mountain into a molehill.

Gearing up to press on

One of the hardest parts of growing in the walk for Christ is the part when you have to go it alone at times when family is not seeing the walk. All you know is it can't be shared because you are at a place most people would rather look at through rose colored glasses. That is when you dig in the trenches of your heart and keep pressing on to the light. It will be worth it. I know because I have experienced it and so can you.

One is to create a bridge of coming together as a nation of people with one common goal: to make life better in many ways to help stop the Governmental Post Traumatic Stress Disorder. by praying for the 45th president. That will also help to fix lots of things. Doing this with cupid's bow and arrow is one element we will use.

There are too many people falling prey to the snap fool affect that sends them to the level of the dieconomie. It is time to use the snap out of it affect to stop and look and go the other way instead of being used by Satan. The snap run can be used to protect one's self also from what you may do and the stay out of the way snap to keep you from doing the wrong thing about whoever is at fault.

The use of your snap faith can be a part of the hero in you for you or someone else. The Lord can see to that. Trust him with your reactions. He can use them for good. Then ask him to keep you inline with his will.

This can be one of the best ways to be gifted to know the freedom to want to avoid getting tricked or tripped up to harm or kill. This is a dark side of life that a doesn't have to be put into your reality.

You can take anything in life and make a reason for it to be right or wrong. But the true measure comes when you defeat the wrong with right.

It is what it is

We can and must learn how to discredit the unnatural force that wants to come against us with truth, wisdom and love.

To see your way out

Why do people want to kill in the first place? It could be 1,000 things and at times some may seem good but to get down to the bottom it is not something mankind was created to do. It became a part of what happened in the Garden of Eden. Therefore, if we fix ourselves and give this contributing factor back in a way the Lord wants us to we defeat the wanting to kill state or level of Satan's dieconomie. We can delete it from our subconscious to clear our conscious. It is always another unless it is self protection. Oh well that is a call I will not include in Satan's dieconomie.

Don't let this be too bright for your sight

You have been invited to become the new activist that has one mission to stay out of the zone that Satan calls his dieconomie that practices the loveoutame principles of peace. This is the spring board of a way to make good things happen in your life and help others do the same. It is like another phase of freedom from Satan's zone that identifies the real enemy and it may not be the one you think it is in the

first place that could be you without you knowing it.
But no longer does it matter once you are free.

If I don't lead the way to show others how we can
discover and conquer old territories to make territories?
Why am I talking or writing about it if I can't get in a
mighty blow for justice such as David did with Goliath?
There are so many Davids out here now they just
need to be pointed in the right direction to take down
some of the negativity in self first.

The correct pronunciation is Galayath.

Just say "no" to glorify the way to hell

People need to stop thinking they get glorified when
they go to hell. That is right it has had too many
examples such as James Cagney, the actor blowing
himself up saying he is on top of the world or
something crazy and he looks like a fool that headed
to the bottom of hell. Nothing or no one is worth this
kind of ending of a life and you know I am right.

The gangster that says I am not going to be taken
alive. The crooks also who robbed and killed that said,
"I am not going to be taken alive."

The modern day fool who thinks they will make a
name for themselves that will last. O my God, the list
goes on and it is senseless. So get with the
loveoutame change. It is a way out of darkness.

To the misguided at heart: get back on track

There are so many mis-developed friendships that start with someone abusing themselves in a way of not knowing the power of knowing no. That is right now because some people's biggest enemy becomes self. They do not want to believe in "no." People must know that it is Satan working and learn to love the word "no."

There is a fact that it is so understated in a way. It made some of leaders of our nation inspire me to write a book titled, *The Power of Knowing No.* It teaches people how to say no and to know themselves. If more men said no to and stop trying to make someone accept their Advancement, there would be lots less harm to more people.

Cause me to write about this.

You could say one of the greatest battles some people may ever get involved with is the battle when you want to learn whether there is love for you between someone else and yourself. You find out that there is a battle between you and yourself. You put the other person in between that and they have no way of responding properly. You get angry at them because you are not able to get an answer from them that you want. Actually, you need to be getting an answer from yourself first place. It is no and that is unacceptable and someone seems to get lost out of reality. They feel that you are owed something by someone else.

You are really owed something by yourself and when they want to leave you in that battle alone. You turn around your understanding and get angry at them and want to harm them because they want to exit stage right. You want them to not exit and stay in the fight and it's not their fight in the first place. It raises hell to a degree where it causes devastation and abuse. It may get violent and maybe the next thing you know it is a ball of confusion that you can't get out of because of what is more than a spiritual war. You may have a schism that adds to the problem that you had in the first place. Of course it is the opposite then you have a double indemnity of damnation in the non relations, whether it ended or never was in the first place.

Remember to learn how to not have battles with yourself in the first place. Say no before you get involved. Then you will not have to get involved with a battle with someone else. In other words, don't fight for nothing when there's nothing really worth fighting for. Leave things alone and people alone. Get the love you need for yourself before you try to include anyone else in your life.

Muse news

Nothing I do is worth the paper it is written on unless it is shared with someone who can learn from it.

Muse news

As time goes on Satan keeps retooling. This is a part of the Lord's retooling program because he will always stay steps ahead of Satan.

Muse news

It is neither here nor there but at the same time was having closer to the earth than ever before or afterwards when the Lord took the tower down.

Muse news

The books I write are not for entertainment purposes. They are to help people improve their life to get it on a more happy, healthy and secure place in the spiritual realm of things. This will allow the state of life to become more wholesome.

Muse news can become very useful

To make it plain and simple, the government gives tax breaks or so they say but they only go so far.

Moving on to a new kind of momentum

Know that nowhere else can you get these kinds of breaks I am talking about. After you join the Lord's dream team the Father, Son and Holy Ghost there are a lots of deductions. No worrying or depression; you do not have to lie. You do not have to steal. You do not have to kill. You do not have to be foolish. You do not have to be crazy. You do not have to be lazy and the list goes on and on. So who has the best deductions when you compare mankind's to what the Lord has to offer?

Muse news

Know that our differences can be our strengths.

Muse news

Time is a friend to all things good and what a friend to have in writing. It gets better every day.

Muse news

Rest on the edification of this scroll.

Muse news

Know that giving makes a lot of people happy. Try it; do not judge.

You know that new words that begin with "schism" can cause you to become a snap fool to increase sickness, flat-out or right out to the road to sinning.

Are the books something the Lord wants you to have?

Why do people's kill? They are out of control. This can come from something bad that happened in someone's life that is a part of trauma. It can sicken people to make them hate and/or act full of foolishness, temporarily insanity, or being somewhat crazy. They may act like a predator or a terror.

The pain some people have is because the devil makes use of if we do not stop it. It is at least self-predicted or predictable. It all does not matter if people had to fix all of this kind of stuff in their life. God gives the power to stop the madness to get control. You can be all that others are and then some in a good way.

If you are in control you won't kill. Let yourself be used by the power of the Lord to protect you from doing wrong things. Then everyone can know how much love you are capable of showing to help keep you going in the right direction in life.

Keep it real

People can stop using their ignorance as an excuse to be a fool and be proud of it at the same time. That is what happens after some people have done the wrong thing. They want to own up to it to so-called protect themselves from whatever may come their way next. It is a part of the old blindness that keeps out of sight to steal the daylight from so many people. It disappears and never returns again to the lives of the innocent to harm them can be stopped.

What is the best tool? Faith, belief and the imagination to work on fixing inner torment to the level of using spiritual skills. It becomes a wrap to not exist in the emotions of one's self and it remains harmless. It is a place that puts begins after the discovery of who you really are, with the news that has come upon your life.

It is better to know of the Lord's next stop when he returns back to earth. You can also wait there at a place in the heart.

This is the process of returning home if you have been lost outside of yourself or inside of yourself. It means to be home on or in a place called Zion. It is a place inside of your heart that you can find a haven of rest, peace and love to go there as if you were a lost sheep who has found their way home. It is heaven's gift to refresh you.

If this news is coming from one of the greatest locations in the nation to show the world who does not know where the greatest location in the world is. It is inside of their heart. Then the loveoutayou has always been there. There are so few who know or there are so many more who need to know.

Foresight to become complete

As the wise men traveled together they shared the knowledge of the world. This is why the book shares some of the same knowledge to make it better for everyone. In *The Biggest Collar* you will find some of the information to help people grow healthier in life. All you have to do is look for the two wise signs. It is only a few chapters in the back of the book but it may put a new light on the light you can see already in this book.

Each book is named after the three wise men: 1. Caspar. He was the king of India and it goes with *The Biggest Collar*. 2. Melchior. He was the king of Persia and it goes with *#Enough*. 3. Balthasar. He was the

king of Arabia and it goes with *Help to Stop Bullies'*
Bullets.

To All

Whether you do or don't go into a house of God you
can get something good out of this knowledge.

So if people do not want to be in fellowship it might be
that they have not so good self-leadership skills. If
you want to get a quick fix for this process learn to
follow the Lord, he is the real leader. Read more
about this. Jeremiah 17:9 can give you some
information on that. Know that at the end of life the
value of life is determined by how much of it was
given away. How much are you giving away? Are you
giving away enough?

A good set of starter tools can be found at Galatians 5:
6. Yet another place you can read up on this
information is John 13:35. A platinum rule is a peace
offering for towers to even get the lost sheep in
Towers out of the devil's lair. To be so saved saved
by the Lord but at the same time leading people to
suffer has a price to be paid. If it is a kind of gateway
to the falling into Satan's trap for others that may lead

to hell. For them the blame will not be the same like the thief on the cross.

I have set up the level of knowledge in this book to reflect three in one book.

To anyone who would like to know what all my writing is about. It is about defeating and helping to stop the injustice on all levels to help people stop being used by Satan. You can be used by Satan in all kinds of ways some of which you may know, some you may not. It is only the shepherd in me that causes me to do as my Father in heaven would do (Isaiah 53:2-6).

There were other wise men that visited Jesus after he got to be an adult. Was one of them connected to my spiritual DNA? To be honest I think we all are if we are believers. Why did they go to Jesus? it was probably to create for clarity in the direction of their gift with a better understanding about it and its use.

I tried to write this book as a very well developed opera so people can sit back and enjoy it and be able to relate to how it may help their life through enlightenment. I will testify that I believe I could be one connected to the spiritual realm that adds to what I am doing. I hope it helps you also.

I am not a perfect human but this level of life helps stop lots of drama and negativity, so it does not affect my spirit and heart. That gives me stability on a healthy and wise growth pattern.

It seems as if I was walking in someone else's shoes when I first started the reread to this book. At the same time it seems as if I hadn't read this book life would have been a little more terrifying in some ways.

After reading this book, we are now ready to imagine that we are in a new era of a birth canal, a spiritual birth canal as a child that will come out. As a child of Christ as we enter into the world the only thing that we need to cry about is the light that shines so brightly that it harms the child. It may not be the fear that harms the child because of being born in sin that causes them to cry.

Now we are being reborn in a spiritual nature where spiritual reality and the light is the thing that affects us in a good way. It is the Lord's light that we see once we come out of a dark pathway. So if we cry it is a good thing not a bad thing.

We claim victory over the healing power that we receive. We come out with our arms open to the world and the love that it has for us. The love that we are going to return to will cause us to claim victory over spiritual illnesses. We claim victory over mental illnesses. God knows if you have a physical illness you may find possible cure but definite victory over that also, in Jesus' name. This is our new present day stance that we take as children of God.

They say that love is better the second time around. Could this be guarantee with God only? Sometimes the earthly love we find with each other can be sweet and sometimes bitter. The Lord's love is always enduring with the sweetness of the fragrance out of a flower. It is the loveoutame flower that blossoms and grows throughout anyone's life who is ready to accept it. This flower that the Lord offers us should be accepted by all so we can plant flowers in a Garden of Eden one day ourselves that he will allow us to go in without being harmed by the Cherubims. Hallelujah.

To cover every base that you can in protecting yourself, make sure that you get a check up on an annual basis for your health care. Something as you might think as insignificant as having low blood sugar can increase your anxiety. It can increase your tenseness and cause you to evolve into some kind of radical individual. It affects your nervous system to a certain degree to protect you from any possible kind of negative feelings of emotions that have become a place in your physical being. It can possibly even affect you to a degree where it is tough teaching in a negative spiritual realm. Keep your blood sugar at a normal level thank you.

Let's get our glucose levels in balance. When those levels are not balanced it depletes energy and causes people to lose self-control. It is a serious issue that we must confront and accomplish so that we will not be addicted to this placement of having an odd system in place. Thank you for caring about yourself because when you care about yourself you care about others. If you can't care about yourself in certain ways you won't care about others. These two negative things may be bound and tied together in ways that cannot be explained but they do exist.

This is a part of the resurrection of life.

The bullet bully sin-drome is a state of being on a Satanic presence of action. It can affect anyone at any time it gets the opportunity to catch someone at a weak state of existence. They are not aware or in control of themselves. The darkness and the power that it possesses overruns the individual who does not have enough light to be able to shine. Their presence of action can be caught up in the unnatural mannerism of harming someone. That is what this is all about, stopping the presence of the darkness over the unknown presents light that is stuck inside of someone. It needs to come out so they would be aware to avoid negativity and obtain and maintain self-control.

Do not be a ding dong because the itch is dead, the itchy witchy finger to pull a trigger itch is dead. Long live the victory of the human race to keep denying a Satanic itch. The itch comes by way of someone who has been taken over by a dead spirit of a warlock or witch. (repeat this three times like a song)

This will give you a possible experience in living that you have been looking for. Without the right information your judgment will be cloudy. This gives you a way of un-clouding your judgment, and gives you an experience for living.

Know that the ceiling and visibility are unlimited. This came from Uncle Bush and it has stood for eons and will stand for eons.

M-N

This is from one bush to another bush to help carry out the wishes of the first bush born between both of us. We hope this develops a kinder and gentler world, from the wisdom that has been placed in writing in this book.

It is nice to know, even if you never met someone they have become a part of your life in a big way. It makes you feel good that there are so many people that you may never know who are alive and have lived.

We're all a big part of a greater plan in preservation for man. It is beginning to look like everyone can contribute a component of love, of presence, of knowledge, of wisdom, of truth and of freedom. We all can rebound back even after we have made a mistake and we came down for whatever reason there may be. So let's give it another chance to become better humans even when we make mistakes, or give ourselves another chance at the truth in it all.

I have made enough mistakes for myself, God knows I have. If I didn't feel he wanted me to give myself another chance, I may have not been here to present what is being unveiled and what is being lifted to give to the Lord as a present within the writing that you are reading. I know he gives everyone one to lift up high in his name.

I can't wait to see what others can do once they find their freedom to do this, even though they may have been in some type of bondage. That doesn't matter anymore because you are free now. Give God his credit while you are on earth and receive his reward when you go to heaven.

New News

The Lord can make a mule talk. This is a part of how to make a person wiser than a mule with enough wisdom to choke a mule. If the Lord can make this happen, can mankind get understanding from it to make one wise if they got a belly full of it.

One of the best parts of this teaching may be the fact that you can catch up with your life again if it has gotten away from you. I testify to the fact that I am thankful to the Lord for helping me get it back before it got lost forever.

A good way to know to go

Now when you close one book you open up another that the Lord had made for you to be a part of your life. The book that gives all written knowledge of what you've done. You do not want to be known as an individual who has taken someone else's life. It may have been a life that the Lord had plans for in a mighty way to do mighty things. That means you have set back his promise but it will get done.

Satan wants to try to eliminate as many things as possible that the Lord can get done. There is a such thing as long-suffering. This long-suffering is when he wants someone to wake up from whatever negative reality they are in. It would only last for a night as he said in and with the crying of the tears in weeping.

When someone does something wrong and they don't repent for it they create a long-suffering situation for themselves and or not forgiving someone they may create a long-suffering for themselves. It is a kind of way of punishing someone in a frame of existence before they have a permanent punishment on their lives.

Remember God doesn't need you to do his work for him on a level of harming someone in need of help. He wants us to know the sickness of others to be able to stop ourselves from taking someone's life. Satan wants a different outcome to create an episode that can ruin your epitaph of what you are going to be in the future. You don't need this on your resume, "I was a murderer for no good reason." Eliminate that chapter in your life you know.

What can I say about this method? I have faith that it will help to deter some people from wanting to commit crime because of a new presence of love. This is the will of the Lord to be a part of something he has put in place to stop sin that leads to crime or crime that leads to sin.

M-N

Say to yourself from time to time, "May the end game of Baal be damned. I will not worship it."

M-N

Laughter is the healing power for corrosive elements in life. Human is the head that shake off any bad tail!

Act I:4-8
4. And being assembled together with them, He commanded them not to depart from Jerusalem, but to wait for the Promise of the Father, "which," He said, "you have heard from Me;
5. "for John truly baptized with water, but you shall be baptized with the Holy Spirit not many days from now."
6. Therefore, when they asked Him, saying, "Lord, will You at this time restore the kingdom to Israel?"
7. And He said to them, "It is not for you to know times or seasons which the Father has put in His own authority.
8. "But you shall receive power when the Holy Spirit has come upon you; and you shall be witnesses to Me in Jerusalem, and in all Judea and Samaria, and to the end of the earth."

This is added to the end of 4 books so that you will know to further your education and teaching. It is time to lay hands on the 20/20. after that one it is ending the world's deadliest sin when it appears in 2019.

To know good news and have patience to use

The main curse of humanity is the poverty of not knowing your spiritual wealth that is not dead. It is worth more than all the material wealth on Earth. If you do not have a presence of understanding about that you are poor and it is the true crime in life. There is no bigger one than to be at a place that has no love that can last forever in one's life. It is really the biggest and only poverty in life no one needs to have and that is why that is what has been happening to people all over the world. So can we change it the face of this problem for the Earth. If you help the Lord make thank you personally I believe can you?

Today here is the opportunity that comes out of or a miracle of understanding

It is my hope that everyone and then some who reads this will have the wisdom to glorify the Lord's word in the flesh to make themselves able to poke holes through the darkness until the light comes through!

News to be used

This may be the Lord's gift but he wants you to unwrap it for him and share in the good of it. In his son Jesus' name, please participate and all are welcome!

The 2020 book is the, or an, eye opener. If we pray to know that what mankind has done it can be forgiven by the Lord then the rest is up to us to see how much good can come out of the work we do to help ourselves and the future generations of the world.

News to be used!

The greatest part of all of this is we are developing a collective forgiveness plan to bring the human race up to a better level of loving one another.

Muse news

The doves of the Lord are released in these books

Explanation has been given.

The 20/20 recovery of the world in preparation of the Lord coming back!

What can be one of the best things learned it is to own up to our responsibilities no matter how small or large and or but to also never leave out love.

New News Center

Now it is time to know when you do not have to mean harm to be harming people so think about what you may not need to do and do not do it.

The four books are in agreement they are somewhat as one that can be known as The Four Seasons mixed on whatever level that comes to one's mind it is your choice: winter, spring, summer or fall. The presence of "I can weather the weather, whatever the weather." In order to help put a stop to all kinds of 1. massive killing, 2. single killing, 3. two dual killing, 4. self killing. Time is not out time is in for living a full life, as was meant to be for everyone the Devil is a Lie to be one of the Lost with adding to his the economy. His lie has exposed.

The books I have written are like team players. Every time you read another one, you add more of you as a member to the body of Christ.

Muse news times 2

That what can't kill you can make you stronger if you face up to it and follow the fact that one day you will find your talent and use it so do not fear the next opportunity that will come your way.

Muse news

Remember that in the darkest moments humor is open to your connecting with it. It can be the greatest fun.

Whatever tries to choke you out of life or someone else with the noose around your throat, forget about it. It may be a big pill to swallow but you can. It is not about you it is about a "we thing," because you are not alone. It will take all hands on deck to make some of the things right in this world. All of us may have been tricked or tripped up by a kind of fire and brimstone that harmed us. I am sure in the past I have had hell misery put on me.

It was my cross to bear, no matter how big or little. I had to face up to and bounce back and bear the weight. However, the Lord did help me carry it.

145

We will take the complete dead spirit of all creation and add them up to give a level of how bad the problem of we put out is along with what we have been getting back in America.

Now if you have the presence of being a part of the Godly we movement. This is one of the wise men book titles with the name of Balthasar. It is a preference to the gift for the Lord. That is what it can be to you!

To show up on deck you will need to see a new horizon of schooling. This can be found in the other two books and the book that has a title called The 20/20 vision for the peoples in America's future to be released in 2019. You can email me if you're interested at Bound To Heaven publishing Ministries to get a copy.

Muse news

I will say the wounded make the best soldiers. They have been there and learned to stay out of the way of our enemy and can also teach others. That is why Satan wants to take them out.

To complete this book you may want to read, _The World's Deadliest Sin: Towerism_. After you complete that one it is recommended that you read the book about America's Comeback 2020.

The first three books had to be stopped to let people catch a moment in time, before things got new once again.

Remember to never let lift stop on you because we can never get enough.

I know I can make a mountain out of a molehill as you can when we are in the will of the Lord.

I wound like to introduce you to the Annex of all other four books

It is a book titled:
Ending the World's Deadliest Sin: Towerism
(Starting in the USA then the world)

The four books that this book need to be attached to are: *Help to Stop Bullies' Bullets*, *#Enough, The Biggest Collar* and *The Comeback of America 2020*. These books have a part two that completes the four. I put this in a context like that because it is the last of the knowledge that goes with all of the books. To some people, it can stand by itself. We can say it is like a chess game with this as the last move.

As an example, if you know about the game of chess, and you look at a picture that was painted in 1800s, you see the king has the last move to win the game. It was a novice's turn to move but the other player was a professional. All you could say is it was a great looking picture. This is the same way with life. The king has the last move to check mate and win. So if we know what is good for us we move with him. To see the picture for yourself look up 'one more move chess' on the web to see a picture that is put together to inspire everyone.

Is this another way to look up to the truth we can trust? Now reattach this book to the back of the other ones. Is this also the message to help us detach ourselves from the things that could kill us or others? Keep living for the next move of the king. Life is on and not to be turned of. It is a good time to come out of all darkness. Now it is your move.

Again, reattach this fifth book to the four that add to the grace and truth. See yourself detach from the death of the bones of the collarism or just wanting to be of a human kind of development. And not a spiritual development of a presence in a human existence.

This book has been made of less than one half of the other parts of the four books it goes with. However, it is all for one and one for all.

These are my seeds I am planting for showing up for Christ. If you find some good seeds here, do not look over them, share them.

M-N

We had a process of suffering in life that some want to become normal from. They first need to be healed in a way to stop whatever is wrong, without hesitation.

This is for the good, bad and the ugly, it doesn't matter, to end the war within. If you have ever experienced it, the prayers are open to receive you.

About the author

The level of trauma that I went through in my life and having no one there on somewhat of a one on one basis put me through a kind of living hell. The Lord kept me company thanks to the Holy Spirit and the seeds that was planted by my mother and father also my family, friends, preachers and teachers in ministry.

It is a good feeling to be one to help break the chains of trauma in life. This counterfeit buck stops here. I will not pay it forward. It doesn't get past me. It is my chance to stop and bury a bad part of history that I can be proud of myself for today and always. This can be a swan song to be heard in the hearts of people once they get by the sour notes. What a way to have a new beginning and you better believe it.

Stopping Bullies' Bullets
The killing at schools
The killing at home
The killing in the streets
The killing by police
The killing of self
The killing all kinds
The killer who drives

Take no knock out or drop outs in life of this kind

I have to give thanks to the Lord for allowing me to complete this love offering. It is my honor and privilege to make this love offering to the father God in heaven. I hope he will be satisfied with this and I say Amen and Hallelujah.

149

To see; to know; to show; to love

I like to think that I can stay in the right flying state of mind as if I am practicing an angel dance without falling out of control. If I don't feel good about my conscious and emotional level at times I can spin myself and wish the cares of what maybe troubles away. I can do this over and over again as I go around and around. It frees me from the harm that wants to consume me with negativity. So I encompass myself and become a big spinning top myself. If I get tired of spinning myself around before the unhealthiness stops, and/or until it does, I can use my little spinning top which is also a therapy toy.

To help myself, at the same time, if I have a negative state of thought to go with the emotional and physical side using the release of the mental side of a self-healing therapy to help stop pressure from going through my halo, it can free me from what I do not want to think about that is wrong.

You can sit back and use your imagination to see yourself spinning around and around. You will know you are free from a sin debt that Satan wants you to incur.

The thought of the process of negativity going up through the halo outside of my thoughts and dissipating and disappearing forever is what will be considered a release valve to get the pressure out. It is a God given therapy that man is allowed to use with faith to guide all people to a pathway of righteousness.

150

At the same time, I am getting my healing with my spiritual skills, my mental and physical with this kind of food. I am taking care of my mind and soul by releasing the cupid in me and the Godly part of the arrows to target all so I can share the loveoutame, as I go about my life to show how I can feel good about myself and others around me!

This is God's way of helping all people get a full recovery of the wounds of pain and hurt on all levels in life peoples are exposed to. It even helps the towerists slide down out of the towers, big ones or little ones. Now the way out is made to stop the fear of harming one's pride as they slide down or come down and grow up instead of trying to fake it as if they have some kind of power and guardianship over others, along with being released from Satan's toehold and the noose, if it got that far.

To help anyone understand more about the prolific surrounding this therapy you can find all the additional details in the book, *Ending The World's Deadliest Sin: Towerism*.

Does mankind still refuse to
become aware of this truth?

This is a collage of information from
one of the next books I will be releasing.

It can also help with spiritual growth.

151

The Good News

We now can understand Satan so all that is left to do is resist him and he will flee from your presence. This is a better way to use your time in a day to make Satan go away.

Know this: Satan doesn't change. What stopped him one thousand years ago still does it today. We were made to break it from its routine.

Stop the killing fields. Make no more makeshift memorials along the streets or home front

It is a fact that there are a lot of individuals who do not understand that love comes with a live and die part of a relationship that may want you to harm a spouse or friend of a spouse. This can happen once a relationship comes to an end. These are, or can be, some of the most harmful feelings because they develop hatred towards someone you love or someone who loved you once. The hatred comes in when you are not loved anymore. This is another serious issue that we deal with in society.

Learn how to not become a hater when someone who harms the one they want to love them or the one they want to continue to love them and they want to continue to love, but it doesn't happen. It becomes a blinding spot that can drive someone crazy, if they let it, by not looking for the light from one of the many son roof tops that is open if you. Learn to look up at the stars at night from time to time and know there is great love for you to receive. Remember, you have to humble yourself first.

It is time to learn about your spiritual grid and examine it. It is time to explore it. It is time you ventured out into it to see what it truly has to offer you. It is a place where you can discover a new meaning of life, a new meaning of reality, a new meaning of spirituality and heavenliness. It may also be a place to discover how to walk through a black hole or dog spot because they can be illuminated with light.

Stop and hear this with your heart

Little of this may be known by many, the spiritual grid and how it functions in our daily lives. We know there is more to it than meets the ears and heaven knows the part of it that meets the eye.

We can discover as much as we would like if we meet within our hearts and minds to express our concern and to manifest righteousness through understanding and growth within the spirituality of our existence as mere humans.

This can be a quest for a new dimension in time and space that may be an existing right before your eyes and you are not aware of it. Now you cannot only become aware of it but be a part of the process to utilize it so that you can discover new avenues and open new doors and conquer new things that need to be conquered in your life and teach others how to do the same with theirs.

An awakening is taking place and there is a migration for this level of achievement this level of education this level of maturity in this land and other lands throughout the world.

Thank you for at least entertaining the thought of presenting yourself with a new stage to be presented on so that not only the earthly principles and people that develop ethical sincerity will know who you are but the heavenly body will also.

We are being watched as if we are in a play on a stage. Our performance can be somewhat astounding first to our own pattern of developing the spiritual guidance, then to the connection and unification throughout our existence on earth and our connection in heaven. Thanks to God Amen and Hallelujah that we can enjoy this new way of maturing and becoming fulfilled in a holistic way.

God has given us a new measure of love that will allow us to redefine our spiritual being on a level to his likeness and not the one that Satan may have developed in you, but a new measure of love that will allow us to really define our spiritual DNA level to his likeness and not the one that Satan may have developed in you.

Forever comes today and that is a good day.
Be prepared for it.

Now anyone and everyone can see into Satan's cloak of darkness. You can see him being stripped and unveiled of all of the demonic presence and his power being taken away by the truth that is setting people free from different bondage on all levels and stopping individuals by the multitude from going into bondage and destroying nations of people at the same time. This is truly one of God's miracles that has been manifested into existence.

What may be America's biggest job it is to clean up the spiritual cesspool that has been trying to erupt like a volcano on the land for last hundreds of years that America has been in existence.

People who have towerism are full of bull because they have the illusion of principles of hanlon's razor (never attribute to malice that which is adequately explained by stupidity) that some may be living by unknowingly. Maybe the next book can be titled "Closing Hanlon's Razor," basically because it came out of opening a kind of Pandora's Box. We can put a stop to it with the use of cupid's arrows.

Now what is Satan's biggest or one of his greatest assets? It is for people to not know when they are wrong and doing the wrong thing. He keeps them wise to unknowing wisdom.

They are blind to not knowing or seeing in some cases to keep them thinking they're right when they're wrong, not having any idea that they're wrong. They can blindly be laid into his sin nature of an untrue, unseen force of reality that makes them want to believe they are accomplishing something on a positive level. In a lot of cases they're not so much what can be said about this as something that we have to take out of the contents of reality and put into the contents of reality.

What I mean is, do not be blinded yourself. Leave it by your blindness without being consciously or woke to it. Should we call this an awakening also out of a darkness that has led someone's or so many to the?

These are the no more slaughterhouse rules that are being set in place by understanding the stupidity that doesn't look like it's stupidity, with bad rules of blindness that come along with everything else out of Pandora's Box we have just dumped out to be seen by mankind.

Acts 20:24 – But none of these things move me; nor do I count my life dear to myself, so that I may finish my race with joy, and the ministry which I received from the Lord Jesus, to testify to the gospel of the grace of God.

Philippians 4:17 – Not that I seek the gift, but I seek the fruit that abounds to your account.

If you have ideas to share, contact Tracy Bush via email, tb.bthpm@gmail.com.

www.ingramcontent.com/pod-product-compliance
Lightning Source LLC
Chambersburg PA
CBHW070833310526
45788CB00017B/559